Other *LightLines Publishing* titles:

BOOKS

The Lost Steps of Reiki: The Channeled Teachings of Wei Chi
by Thomas A. Hensel & Kevin Ross Emery

Combing The Mirror (and other steps in your spiritual path)
by Kevin Ross Emery

Experiment Earth: Journey Back To The Beginning
by Kevin Ross Emery & Thomas A. Hensel

Invisible Armor: Protecting Your Personal Energy
by Thomas A. Hensel

AUDIO TAPES

The Lost Steps of Reiki: Transforming An Ancient Healing Art
by Thomas A. Hensel & Kevin Ross Emery

Prosperity & Manifestation
by Thomas A. Hensel & Kevin Ross Emery

The Channeled Messages of Simon Peter
by Thomas A. Hensel & Kevin Ross Emery

COMPACT DISCS

Creating Your Invisible Armor
with Thomas A. Hensel

Managing
The
Gift

Alternative Approaches For Attention Deficit Disorder

Dr. Kevin Ross Emery

LightLines Publishing
Portsmouth, NH

Managing The Gift:
Alternative Approaches For Attention Deficit Disorder

First Edition, 2000

Published by:

LightLines Publishing
PO Box 5067
Portsmouth, NH 03802-5067

E-mail: LightLinesPub@aol.com
Website: http://www.weboflight.com/publish.htm

Manufactured in Canada

ISBN 1-890405-21-3

Dedications

First and foremost, to my "kids" from three to one hundred and three that have let me share their lives and made this journey worthwhile. When I see these A.D.D. "kids," it gives me so much hope for their future, my future and the future.

To Tommy, who keeps showing up when I need him most and loving me even when I am most unlovable.

And to my research assistant, Suzanne, who with the tenacity of a bulldog made sure I had access to all the latest information, newest thoughts and greatest controversies about this subject.

<u>*Acknowledgements*</u>

No book is ever written alone, and a book like this shares not only my views and experiences on Attention Deficit Disorder but those of all the people who were impacted who came through my life. And not only them, but also their families, friends, employers and educators. I heard from them all.

So here is the list, first names only (to protect the innocent and the guilty) of the people I would like to thank for their input into this project: *David, Cody, Bill, Adam, Mathew, Laura, Ryan, Peter, Elaine, Donna, Kelly, Stephen, Eric, Sean, Brandon, and so many more that I cannot even begin to name.*

Thank you to *Jim & Louise Simms* for opening the door.

Then there were those who were part of the "edit by committee" who gave input, feedback, and hauled me in when I got too carried away.

First, my two professional editors:
Lesley Weisbrot & Hillary Smith

And then the committee:
*Tommy Hensel, Tricia Dawson, Carol Looney,
Jacqui Tinsley, Suzanne Koenig and Del Skillins.*

Thanks, one and all, for your love, support and patience.

Dr. Kevin Ross Emery
Portsmouth, NH
August 2000

Table of Contents

Managing The Gift

Alternative Approaches For Attention Deficit Disorder

Introduction

I sat and reread the e-mail one more time as I began to reflect. I was remembering the first contacts I made with this child impacted with Attention Deficit Disorder. The e-mail brought tears to my eyes as I read:

> *I want to tell you and others what has helped our son become a more receptive person about his A.D.D. Coming into our home and working with him, you enlightened him about many facets of himself. But the one thing that he has pronounced as being the most important is that he accepts the fact he learns differently and he has to work at focusing on one particular thought and process at a time. Since he has accepted this, his whole life has turned more positive. He asks many questions in the classroom. He tells teachers and other students he realizes he is no longer stupid—he is different and that is okay. More importantly, he tells himself he is not stupid and that his brain works differently than other kids do.*
>
> *Guess what? He made all As and Bs this six weeks and his self-esteem and self-confidence is at an all time high. He has set himself a schedule just like you told him to do. He does his homework as soon as he gets home*

from school, taking small breaks to let his mind wander. He takes his time and, if frustrated about not knowing how to do something, he stops for five minutes, regroups and begins again.

His reward is the most precious thing ever for himself and his family: the wonderful smile he had when handing out his report card. He went off the Ritalin after your counseling and asks me at least once or twice a week when he can see you again. He misses you deeply and looks up to you as the 'Dude' that truly understands and knows what is going on in his brain. You gave him guidance and something his father and I did not know how to do. You gave him back the love he has for himself.

You have helped our child to get off the medication that he hated taking and we hated to have him on. And you helped this child move from a child the teachers complained about with a C- average to a child that the teachers are now saying is a model student and who is on the honor role.

We thank you from the bottom and top of our hearts and love you very much.

I remember the frustration of the parents who knew their child was not stupid and the frustration of the child who did not know how to access the intelligence he had. I remember the moment when I started to explain to him what was really going on in his brain—what it felt like, what it looked like and how it worked—and he burst into tears. I remember him begging me not to tell his parents just how different he was because they would never to be able to love him if they knew.

How many times have I heard that from both children and adults—the fear, the isolation, the frustration about this thing we call Attention Deficit Disorder? How many times have I heard the confusion obscuring this thing we are quick to medicate and resistant to understand? Let's look at a few of the outstanding questions that surround Attention Deficit Disorder.

Attention Deficit Disorder (A.D.D.). What is it? Where does it come from? Did the increase and overload of information create it? Can it really be cured by diet? Is medication the only answer? Am I being a bad or neglectful parent if I do not medicate my child? Does A.D.D. have to play out negatively in my relationship? Is there any such thing as A.D.D. or is it a created condition? Is it a gift? If so, why?

I will cover these and many more questions in this book. I will begin with the 'short answers.' You must then read the detailed explanations later in this book. Next, I will share how I came upon my journey of doing work to help people learn how to understand and manage the gift of A.D.D. First, however, the short answers:

What is it?

Attention Deficit Disorder is a name we have given to the increased visibility of certain aspects of our evolution as a species. It is also a name that has been assigned to many other things that may or may not have to do with that evolutionary process.

Where does it come from?

It is evolutionary in nature and stems from our ability to grow and change as a species.

Did the increase and overload of information create it?

Although the A.D.D. impacted person has been on the scene for quite some time, the number of people with the impact has increased. Because of the brilliance of these people, there has been an increase of technology and information. This condition helps more children and adults access dormant abilities.

Can it really be cured by diet?

There are certain dietary sensitivities. Sometimes they only appear when there are excesses of those foods in the diet. Other times these foods are just toxic to the system. In both cases, these sensitivities can manifest themselves as undesirable behaviors within the A.D.D. impacted person. Attention to diet and such sensitivities can decrease, if not eliminate, some of the behavioral excesses. Changes in diet, however, cannot 'cure' A.D.D. In itself, it is not something that is curable, nor would you want to cure it.

Is medication the only answer?

No. Most of the time it is not even a good one.

Am I being a bad or neglectful parent if I do not medicate my child?

Decisions need to be based on what is best for your child, not what is best for the schools or easiest for the child's caretakers. Depriving children from parts of themselves to make them easier to deal with sounds more abusive than good or attentive.

Does A.D.D. have to play out negatively in my relationship?

No. With some mutual work and understanding, it can be quite the positive and even desirable thing to have in a child or a partner.

Is there any such thing as A.D.D. or is it a created condition?

Attention Deficit Disorder is simply a condition that is often identified by the following series of symptoms: being easily distracted, an inability to focus, impulsive actions and hyperactive behavior. If A.D.D. is what we are going to call this, then the answer is "Yes, sometimes it exists by itself." Other times what we have labeled as A.D.D. is actually poor diet, poor parenting, poor educating, emotional traumas, other conditions or some combination of all of the above.

    If I were to name the condition of many of the people being labeled A.D.D. myself, I might try something more like

C.I.S.—Cultural Inconvenience Syndrome. I would call it this because the people who are impacted by A.D.D. are often inconvenient to the culture that surrounds them. Instead of identifying the problem as being system-based, the culture in general finds medicating these people to be the answer. Also, there are people who have many other issues going on which fit into the same C.I.S. labeling. It is just easier to let them all be medicated; it is just more convenient.

Is it a gift? If so, why?

Yes, it is a gift. As you read this book, I will show how A.D.D. is a gift in each of the four levels (physical, emotional, intellectual and spiritual). In an ideal setting, one which is well developed and well understood, the attributes of the person impacted with A.D.D. would be appreciated in many different ways. The person would have more energy with less food and be more able to understand and process their emotions in a healthy way. Their intellect would be more accessible to them and they would realize the ability to make great intellectual leaps while thinking in both an analytical and abstract way. This, in turn, would allow them to be more intellectually efficient in their thought processes. Finally, the person would be more spiritually aware of their connection to everything around them—from the planet to all things, humans included, that live upon the planet.

If this is the kind of person you would like to be, perhaps now can understand A.D.D. is a gift.

****

Now that I have given you some of the short answers, let me tell you how I came about this journey. First, let me share with you how I do my work. I am a spiritual coach and counselor. I have worked with many different gifts that people would identify as psychic. My own gifts came to me at an early age: being able to 'know' or 'see' things that most people did not. The journey through my gifts and abilities, which often separated me from my peers, has been a lifetime journey. Never have I felt that information that has been endowed to me has been so profound or important to the future as the information I have received and am still receiving on the subject of Attention Deficit Disorder (A.D.D.). Both my intuitive gifts and my life experiences came together to prepare me for this part of my journey.

The intuitive part of my journey began when I was four and my Grandmother first talked to me about my gifts. She said to me: "Kevin, you have a gift from God. People will tell you that you are wrong, or bad or that they do not believe you. As long as you know that it was a gift from God, everything will be alright." My journey had begun.

That journey has taken me many places and led me to the work I do now as a teacher, spiritual coach and spiritual counselor. I have helped people become more empowered, make better decisions, release old habits and patterns, separate themselves from negative influences and become more aware of themselves as spiritual beings. I am a rebel by nature and that is sometimes what I consider my greatest gift. I will not accept something as 'so' simply because it has either always been done that way or because an 'authority' has declared it as truth.

As I mentioned before, my life experiences also prepared me for the work I am doing on A.D.D. When I was five years old, during the last half of the school year, my parents received a note concerning my placement in class. They were informed that, on the recommendation of my teacher, the school would like to put me in a class with kids who needed extra help learning. In those days, it was called the 'slow class.' My father and mother decided that the three of us should have a meeting with the teacher and the school before making that decision, as they did not have the impression that I was 'slow.'

My parents asked why the school felt I should go into a special class. They were told that, when a question was asked in class, I often put up my hand, but when called on I would either trip over the answers, put the words in the wrong order or could not get the answers out. Upon hearing this, my father had me sit on his lap. He told the teacher to ask me a question. The teacher complied and when I started to answer, I did everything the teacher had described until my father intervened. He told me to stop, take a deep breath and think about what I wanted to say. When I did this, I answered perfectly and correctly! I continued to do so for the next several minutes for every question they asked me. Whenever I would start to get excited, my father would get me to stop, center, breathe and then respond. My father concluded that the problem was that I thought too fast and I had too much information I was trying to share all at once. He then concluded that I was not slow, that I was actually too bright for my own good. What I needed was a teacher for smart kids, not 'slow' ones.

Needless to say, I was never put into the 'slow' class. I spent most of my school years with very good grades and in above average classes. I even graduated after the first half of my senior year and started college in January. I already had my first semester of college done when I walked down the aisle to get my high school diploma.

My work helping people with A.D.D. began early in 1999. My primary practice was doing *Combing The Mirror*™ coaching.[1] Among my clients were a married couple for whom I was doing marriage coaching and counseling. One day after we had been working together for several months, the husband came in and announced that, at the age of 67, he had just figured out that he had A.D.D. Because of that discovery, many things had started to make sense.

Once he made that announcement, I looked at him as I might look at someone while performing a medical intuitive scan. Then I 'saw' it. I 'saw' the way the A.D.D. affected him. The things that had seemed 'irrational' and had plagued him his whole life were no longer without reason. The rages, the problems with alcohol, relationship issues and even some of the survival skills he had developed now made sense. These were the things that drove his wife crazy—things that he could not help.

---

[1] *Combing The Mirror coaching*™ is a system of coaching and spiritual counseling based upon the book *Combing The Mirror (and other steps in your spiritual path)* by Rev. Kevin Ross Emery (©1998, LightLines Publishing).

As I started to describe what I was seeing, he verified that some of these revelations had been referred to in the book on A.D.D. that he had been reading; however, I was also getting more information and in more depth. Before I was finished, he knew I truly understood how he felt and what was going on within his brain. Between the book and the information I retrieved, we began to create an understanding between his wife and himself that then began a renaissance within the marriage. We created protocols which 'managed' the impact without sacrificing the gift, all without medication.

At the close of that first session I took a couple of notes and thought about how interesting the information had been. I assumed that, except for working with this particular couple, my A.D.D. work was finished. This was on a Wednesday. That Friday, I received a call from a woman who had been studying *Wei Chi Tibetan Reiki*™ with me.[2] Her son, whom I will call Bobby, had been having problems with the school system. He had been diagnosed with A.D.D. among other things and the school system was really pushing her to medicate him. Neither she nor Bobby wanted to do that, but the situation had been getting progressively worse. Now Bobby had begun talking about how it would be 'easier to die' and that 'no one understood.' On the day she called me, he had run away from school. Did I think I could help him? I told her I would try.

Meeting Bobby, I could immediately see the young man's pain. I said to him, "I can see you are in a great deal of pain. Can you tell me why?"

He told me, "It hurts me to be a human when I see and think of all that we have done to this planet. But I know I am here to make it better."

'Looking' at Bobby from an energetic perspective, it was as though he had been born without skin, feeling everything that went by him. I shuddered at the thought of what it would be like to be born without skin, without boundaries. By the end of my

---

[2] *Wei Chi Tibetan Reiki*™ is a form of Reiki which dates back five thousand years to the Tibetan monasteries. More information is available in *The Lost Steps of Reiki: The Channeled Teachings of Wei Chi* by Rev. Thomas Hensel and Rev. Kevin Ross Emery (© 1997, LightLines Publishing).

first session with this young man, I clearly knew: A.D.D. was not a disability, it was a gift—a gift that would need to be managed and nurtured, but a gift nonetheless. It is where we as a species are evolving. If we continue to medicate our future, we risk losing that future. In that first session, I saw so much about why these people are special. I realized that my information was sometimes specifically about Bobby and sometimes about the impact in general.

Many people wonder, when I talk about Bobby, why I saw his being born without skin as a gift. In seeing him and all his wisdom, there was a beautiful innocence and love for all things created by God. But I knew that you can always teach someone how protect themselves; you cannot, however, always take someone who is born with barriers and teach them how to let them go—how to face the fear and be. Bobby knew how to be; he just did not know how to shield.

As more people diagnosed with A.D.D. began to 'show up' on my doorstep, more and more things became clear to me. Some of the people falling under that category of 'die hard,' the ones who were diagnosed years earlier, know all the terminology and are masters at what I now call 'A.D.D. Speak.' They know the jargon. These people are sometimes the most difficult to educate because they have grown so comfortable with the meaningless labels that they have been given. For them, the label provides a box into which to fit themselves. I have to convince them to step outside of the box. I am aware of how safe that box can be, and how scary the world can feel to the person with A.D.D.

Just as we all are unique, the way A.D.D. affects each person is different. It is not unusual to encounter more than one diagnosis for these people. This makes the work challenging for both the practitioner and the client. In this book, I will not be able to perfectly shadow your experiences, but I can offer you suggestions and actions to help you with the journey.

Chapter 1
Framework

An old boss of mine, whenever he began to train some-one on something new, would always say, "Let us make sure that we are all singing off the same sheet of music." Since there is a training aspect to this book, I think that would be a good place to begin. So let us make sure we are singing off the same sheet of music.

I would like to begin by sharing a few basic truths to which I will refer as I proceed through the book. Let's begin with the word 'truth.' When I refer to something as truth, unless otherwise stated, I am speaking about *my* truth. This first concept is an extremely important one. Information is too often presented as **THE TRUTH**, when in fact it is either a truth someone has learned from someone or somewhere else, or it is their personal truth based on their experiences. Personal truths run rampant in A.D.D. work. I have often reviewed information concerning A.D.D. where things are being presented as truth when they are really opinion. Much damage could be and probably has been done by stating opinions as truth. Sometimes the deliverer of a truth really believes what they say. Other times they intentionally desire to lead you towards a conclusion that will benefit them. I will elaborate on some of my truths in this chapter, though most of them will be detailed in several places where they are most relevant. You will see more and more why I say they are truths:

1. A.D.D. is a *diff-ability*, not a disability.
2. The A.D.D. label is limiting, dangerous and it creates additional problems for the individual.
3. Easily changed or managed outside factors can have a profound effect on the A.D.D. person meeting their goals without medication.
4. Incorrect and/or incomplete diagnoses are a regular occurrence.
5. Medication is best used last yet it is overused, recommended first and portrayed as the primary if not only option.
6. Medication hides or obscures other things which are potentially dangerous, harmful and, in some cases, life threatening.
7. Inflexibility, narrow-mindedness, emotional bullying and/or blackmail, incorrectly presented information and laziness on the part of those around the A.D.D. person are all significant contributing factors to the astronomical increase in the use of medication for A.D.D.
8. A.D.D. is an indication of brilliance that the person must be taught how to access in order to utilize their full potential.
9. Isolation is one of the greatest risks for a person with A.D.D. It is created from outside sources and of itself is not a tendency of A.D.D., but of the environment. Unchecked isolation can lead a person who is brilliant to become emotionally unstable and potentially violent.
10. Depression is a dangerous side effect of A.D.D. It can mask or mediate some of the more obvious signs of A.D.D. Depression and medication achieve some of the same unhealthy results for the person with A.D.D.
11. The intuitive is an acceptable process by which information may be derived. This information should neither be

immediately accepted nor denied because it is intuitive.

12.   We risk our future through the 'drugging' of our children.
        If continued, this will lead to major upheavals, chaos and
        the destruction of our world, as we know it.

13.   A.D.D. is a gift that is part of an evolutionary process.

Let us review these truths in more depth.

A.D.D. is a diff-ability, *not a disability.*

One of my clients first gave me the term diff-ability, a
word indicating someone who had a 'different ability' or way of
doing something. As soon as I started working with people
impacted with A.D.D., 'diff-ability' was not only a better description, but also a far more accurate one. In fact, not only did I start
using the term regularly, I also added to the concept. Many times
when dealing with children, I not only explained to the child that
they had a diff-ability (not a disability) but that if there is a disability to be found we might need to look at the world we have
created—a world where there seems to be an inability to support
these people's individuality and uniqueness and where
'mainstreaming' is more important than building self-worth.

A.D.D. is often characterized as evident by inability to
focus and an inability to sit still for long periods of time. Yet
every A.D.D. person has been able to sit and focus, even
hyperfocus, when what they are focusing on can hold their attention. There are different ways in which they learn, process and
focus. Their capacity for boredom is high when dealing with
something in which they have no interest. However, they are not
unable to focus; nor are they *unable* to sit still even though their
need to release energy on a regular basis is increased.

The A.D.D. label is limiting, dangerous and creates additional problems for the individual.

Accepting that you are unable to do something, that you
are not 'normal' and are somehow 'broken' and need medication,

has profound effects on self-worth and self-esteem. It has always amazed me that, while members of the psychiatric and medical communities agree that the power of suggestion can cause people to behave in certain ways, they are still so quick to assign limiting labels that create a 'self-fulfilling prophecy' effect in their patients. This particular Catch-22 is very prevalent around the A.D.D. issue.

Easily changed or managed outside factors can have a profound effect on the A.D.D. person meeting their goals without medication.

Many people have chosen to dismiss the importance of environment, diet, behavior modification, individually created systems & schedules and the use of alternatives when treating A.D.D. You can read many articles about how drugs are 'better'; that such alternatives do not cure A.D.D. First of all, drugs do not cure it either—a good thing, as A.D.D. is not an illness. While most of these alternatives will not stand alone in mediating some of the more difficult outgrowths of A.D.D., they all have a role in helping to relieve some of the side effects caused by either the A.D.D. or the environment within which the A.D.D. person lives. Also, the role modeling of and from the family and messages/ influences from all the environmental factors play a major part in the process of achieving the goals of the person with A.D.D. without having to sacrifice themselves in the process.

Incorrect and/or incomplete diagnoses are a regular occurrence.

When I first came to terms with the concept that I was being directed to work with A.D.D., I also became aware that A.D.D. was a label being given too freely. It is not uncommon for other issues to be going on, but they are covered up or ignored through the medication process for A.D.D. As I began my research into the A.D.D. phenomenon, I discovered a great many misdiagnosed cases from doctors who came up with a corrected diagnosis and patients who discovered the real problem on their own.

Medication is best used last yet it is overused, recommended first and portrayed as the primary if not only option.

It may be a hard sell in America, but medication should rarely be a first choice in treating A.D.D. Not all medicine is bad; some medicine is very good and necessary. However, the medications given for A.D.D. cure nothing. They simply and temporarily control behavior. They do have side effects and, depending on the medication, some of these side effects can be life threatening. The Food and Drug Administration labeling for Ritalin, the drug most often prescribed for A.D.D., includes the warning *"Sufficient data on the safety and efficacy of long-term use of Ritalin in children are not yet available."* The fact that the production of Ritalin has risen over 700% since 1990 is a clear indication of its popularity, at least within the medical community.[1] Members of both the medical and psychiatric community state over and over again that medication is the first, best and (some say) only option.

Medication hides or obscures other things which are potentially dangerous, harmful and, in some cases, life threatening.

In cases where there are other things going on which give the child the appearance of A.D.D., the medication may still mediate some or all of the 'symptoms.' In the meantime, other things such as medical, emotional or dietary problems go unrecognized and untreated.

Inflexibility, narrow-mindedness, emotional bullying, and/or blackmail, incorrectly presented information and laziness on the part of those around the A.D.D. person are all significant contributing factors to the astronomical increase in the use of medication for A.D.D.

The stories of parents fighting back against schools that are 'forcing' them into medicating their children are becoming

---

[1] ABCNews.com in a Nov 16, 1999 interview with Dr Lawrence Diller, author of *Running on Ritalin: A Physician Reflects on Children on Society* and *Performance in a Pill, 1998.*

increasingly prevalent. These school systems say that they do not have funding or resources to deal with the different needs of the A.D.D. child who is not medicated. I, personally, have sat in meetings with school officials where, unless you 'officially' diagnose and follow the recommendations for the diagnosis (i.e. medication), then they are not obligated to do anything special for the child. Yet, many times the desire or convenience factor plays into it. Books from the medical and psychiatric communities often promote the 'bullying' of parents as a teacher's duty. Here is an excerpt from a book which illuminates this:

> *School officials are fond of saying that they don't force parents to put their kids on Ritalin but merely recommend evaluations. However, that is not what many parents say. The pressure some schools put on errant parents who refuse to accept the Ritalin party line is fierce: Parents report being 'ganged up on,' sometimes by five or six school officials at once. Many of these professionals seem to be taking the advice of physicians Edward Hallowell and John Ratey, both firm believers in the 'diagnosis' of A.D.D., who recommend to teachers: "What do you do as a teacher if a parent disregards your suggestions that a child needs an evaluation for A.D.D.? [We] have three solutions to this predicament: persist, persist, and persist. The first no is usually the parents' own denial borne out of guilt. The second no is usually an 'ouch'. The third no usually means, 'I want to say yes if you can only show me how.' So persist. Get support. Don't give up. And give yourself and the parents time. It takes most people a while to change their minds."*

> *What Hallowell and Ratey consider persistence sounds more like brow beating to me. Phrased somewhat differently, their advice is: The teacher is always right, the parent who questions an A.D.D. or hyperactivity label is always*

wrong, and parents must be harassed until they give in and find a doctor who will 'diagnose' A.D.D. or A.D.H.D.[2]

In addition, incorrect and incomplete statements by the largest 'support' organization for people with A.D.D. also contribute to these issues. Children and Adults with Attention Deficit Disorder (CHADD), the nation's largest support group made the following incorrect, misleading or incomplete statements in support of the use of drugs for A.D.D.:

- "Psychostimulant medications are not addictive."
- "The most likely cause of A.D.D. is a chemical imbalance or deficiency in certain chemicals in the brain that are located in the area responsible for attention and activity."
- "Emotional difficulties, including substance abuse, are more likely to occur when a child with A.D.D. is not treated."
- "Medication is not used to control behavior—medication is used to improve the symptoms of A.D.D."
- "Between 70-80% of children respond positively to these (psycho-stimulant) medications."
- "Hundreds of studies on thousands of children have been conducted regarding the effects if psycho-stimulant medications. Relatively few long term side effects have been identified."[3]

We will talk more about CHADD later.

A.D.D. is an indication of brilliance that the person must be taught how to access, in order to utilize their full potential.

When I started to work with this group, my own impres-

[2] Walker, Sydney III. *The Hyperactivity Hoax.* (New York:, St. Martin's Press). Dec. 1998, pp. 213-214.

[3] The Merrow Report *Attention Deficit Disorder: A Dubious Diagnosis?* 588 Broadway Suite 510 New York, NY 10012 Phone: 212.941.8060 Fax: 212.941.8068 Homepage: www.pbs.org/merrow E-Mail: merrow@pbs.org.

sion was one of people with incredible intellect. After researching the subject, meeting with teachers, talking to parents and both children and adults with A.D.D., it became evident that, though this intellect might show up in a generalized way or in one or two primary areas, these people were undeniably brilliant. Someone who has a multi-diagnosis or other mitigating factors may not appear bright. This does not mean some kind of brilliance is not there; but it may be harder to access or it might be highly specialized.

Isolation is one of the greatest risks for a person with A.D.D. It is created from outside sources, and of itself is not a tendency of A.D.D., but of the environment. Unchecked isolation can lead to a person who is brilliant to become emotionally unstable and potentially violent.

When children discover that they are different in ways that no one seems to understand or support, they begin to isolate themselves. When I begin working with someone, the first thing I usually need to do is break through the isolation that they have created-to help connect and dissipate the energies of the internal dialogue which affects their self-worth and their self-esteem. I will investigate the isolation issue in a chapter by itself. Just understand that the emotional effects of A.D.D. have been so unexplored that it has been nearly impossible to help someone with them.

The anger, frustration and emotionally void periods that exist within the A.D.D. person can erupt in a way that is intelligent, well thought out and emotionally disassociated. If left untreated long enough, it can easily play out in violence.

Depression is a dangerous side effect of A.D.D. It can mask or mediate some of the more obvious signs of A.D.D. Depression and medication achieve some of the same unhealthy results for the person with A.D.D.

With the combination of the fear, shame and anxiety that are commonplace among people with A.D.D., depression is not a surprising factor. Instead of becoming outwardly abusive or violent, these people can become inwardly violent and self-abusive.

A depressed child or adult with A.D.D. is less likely to display those behaviors that bring the focus of the system bearing down on them. This is one of the reasons why some children and adults can go undiagnosed or are diagnosed later. Depression will often make a person with A.D.D. fit in better with their peer group or be less obviously inattentive or distracted in a disruptive way. It will also create the same side effects of feeling shut off from one's self—like a zombie.

The intuitive is an acceptable process by which information may be derived. This information should neither be immediately accepted nor denied because it is intuitive.

This is neither the time nor place to get into a lengthy discussion on either the merits or the skepticism concerning psychic abilities. It is sufficient to say there is something that exists beyond the five physical senses. Like any other sense or thought, it can be influenced. Those with a closed mind, I suspect, would not have made it this far. Nevertheless, skepticism is good. Neither doctors nor people with highly developed psychic abilities are God or have all the answers. Both professions have their share of honorable and dishonorable people. The goal here is to apply these truths and the information throughout the book in an open, fair-minded way and see if it helps. There are answers here. You must decide if they are the answers for you or someone you love.

We risk our future through the 'drugging' of our children. If continued this will lead to major upheavals, chaos and the destruction of our world as we know it.

All actions have consequences. Medicating children in larger and larger numbers because they are different, because it is convenient and so that we can hold on to some illusion of normalcy will cause a backlash. Nurturing outdated and outmoded social and educational beliefs will only make the impact of their fall more pronounced, explosive and irrevocable. We are creating a generation, which at some point will revolt against being turned into zombies, cut off from parts of themselves. You may feel that this is a reactionary statement. Historically, however, anytime we have suppressed, imprisoned, or tried to control a certain group of people, they have rebelled.

In 1999, Americans filled more than 11 million Ritalin prescriptions-five times as much as the rest of the world.[4] This does not even include of the other drugs prescribed for A.D.D. The estimated number of children on Ritalin in the US is about 5 million, roughly 70 percent of amphetamine-like drugs prescribed in America. The total amount of amphetamines prescribed for school aged children is around seven million. If we add the two million children on antidepressants to that, it looks as if the number of children on drugs is well over eight million. If these numbers are correct, it means that 15 percent of our children are on psychiatric drugs. This is a very large group. The Journal of the American Medical Association revealed that Ritalin prescriptions for two to four olds increased 200 to 300 percent between 1991 and 1995.[5]   Yet, according to *www.rxmed* (a respected website to get information concerning a variety of drugs), Ritalin, should not be used in children under six years of age. We are risking our future. But keep in mind that drugging is not the only issue. Understanding, working with and supporting, children and adults, impacted with A.D.D. are a few of the other issues that need to be rectified.

A.D.D. is a gift that is part of an evolutionary process.

As I proceed through the book, I will be addressing why the A.D.D. is evolutionary. Keep in mind that at the end of each section of the next four chapters I will talk about why this new

---

[4] Lowe, Carl. *"Paying Attention."* Energy Times, September 1999.
[5] Breeding, John. "Ritalin Use: Simply Out of Control." *Mothering,* No.101. July/August 2000.

way of doing, feeling, seeing and being is a gift. The thing to
remember here is that evolution comes due to many different
factors. As our physical environment and needs have changed, we
have physically changed. As we have become a more intercon-
nected world, our views, our feelings, our thoughts and our
relations to our spiritual development have evolved.

It was not until I had received large pieces of this information that I started to understand the message that I had received
about this being evolutionary. Looking back, I would say that
what we call A.D.D. started coming into the species at a steady
pace about 150 years ago. There have always been a few. Remember that this is an evolutionary process to help us progress as a
species. Many of our 'brilliant, yet erratic' history shapers today
would easily have fit into the A.D.D. mold. So too would many of
what we used to call 'absent minded professor' types, the stereo-
type that did not know when to come in from the rain and had no
common sense. Some of these earlier people, the Edisons, the
Graham Bells, the Einsteins, often had difficulty in school or were
often outsiders—people who were told that they would never
make anything of themselves. They paved the way for today's
modern technology that now, more than ever, plays into the
'distracted' part of A.D.D. I say this because it is the availability
of all this insight and input that makes the A.D.D. person so apt
to become bored in the classroom and the workplace. With more
information then ever before in the history of the world to entice
them, the realities of the outmoded school and work systems
seem particularly boring and uninspiring in comparison.

****

It is time to clarify some terms and concepts with which
you may or may not be familiar. First, let us talk about the concept of the medical intuitive. For many people, the concept of
medical and intuitive would be considered an oxymoron, since
many see medicine as a science and intuition as anything but
scientific. In actuality, many great medical discoveries had more
than a little intuitive jumping involved in the process. The scien-

tific aspect of medicine then had to prove the intuitive leaps after the fact. Oftentimes I wonder if the scientific mind is just there to prove what the intuitive mind knows in order to keep the analytic mind happy.

I do something that I call 'medical intuitive scans' or often, just 'scans.' When I scan someone, I receive information that may include imbalances in the person's energy (which will often correlate to physical imbalances), the cause of particular imbalances and how to correct them. When I do this kind of work, I may either receive information concerning a protocol or I may create one based on the information. A scan may also simply tell me how something is or is not functioning.

When I use the word 'protocol' I am referring to an action plan which can include changes in behavior, habits and patterns. It might also include dietary changes, or the suggestion that the person check in with their medical or holistic practitioner about the use of certain herbs or supplements. Often, we will start the changes slowly, allowing the person to adapt and then adjust things as we go. Now when working with protocols I make it clear that I am not a medical doctor and I cannot diagnose and I cannot prescribe. I merely suggest directions for them to investigate.

One of the other concepts with which I work is that of feminine and masculine energies. These energies are not an indication of gender or sexuality. Everybody has both feminine and masculine energies. When someone is well balanced, they will easily be able to call upon the energy that is most appropriate for the current moment. They are able to shift from masculine to feminine, or feminine to masculine energy at a moment's notice. It is not an intellectual choice. It is the willingness to allow ourselves to go where we are being called without worrying about how it looks or how we think it might be perceived. This and the idea of androgyny both play supporting roles in how and why some of the drama has been born around people with A.D.D. When I refer to androgyny, I speak of someone whose natural state is to be connected to both feminine and masculine energies. I am not saying that the person with A.D.D. is always androgynous, but they are given to being more balanced. This balance can play out in having an androgynous energy about them. If you would like more information concerning feminine/masculine energies and how they play out in everyone's life, then you may want to read my book *Combing The Mirror (and other steps in your spiritual path)*[6] that includes an entire chapter on just this subject. The reason that I bring all this up is that for years I have noticed that more and more children are coming in with a more balanced masculine/feminine energy. This spiritual balancing is a method for a planet that has become very unbalanced in the area of masculine/feminine energy. There is a definite correlation between the two.

When I speak about the environment around the person with A.D.D., I am speaking of their family, school, work and the media. This also includes any social, religious or spiritual groups by which they are influenced. The concept of environment includes all those things that have been a major influence in the shaping of the person's perspective of themselves and the world around them.

When I do a scan on someone with A.D.D., I get information on what is going on in all four of the person's levels. Yes, that's right, four. Every person has one body but four levels. They have a physical level, an emotional level, an intellectual level and a spiritual level. I will do a brief explanation in this chapter and elaborate more about each level in the chapter that is about that particular level.

The *physical level* is self-explanatory. It is your actual physical body. It also is often associated with the physical world around. Therefore, when I talk about the physical level, I am talking about your physical body and your physical world. It includes the actions we take and how we act upon the thoughts and feelings we have. According to many Eastern spiritual and medical systems, certain parts of the physical body house or maintains specific associations with certain emotions and thought

---

[6] Emery, Rev. Kevin Ross. *Combing The Mirror (and other steps in your spiritual path)*. LightLines Publishing, 1998.

patterns. The physical body is also the repository for any ongoing imbalances from the emotional level, the intellectual level or the spiritual level. This concept has existed in many forms throughout all of modern history. Most of us either know or know of a person who is so emotionally distraught that they make themselves sick or someone whose mental thought processes or patterns either directly or indirectly bring them to illness. It is often through the physical body that we receive messages or guidance concerning things that we may or may not be doing but which are parts of our personal spiritual path. We bring 'accidents and illnesses' to us as part of our learning and growing process, but usually only when we have avoided or ignored the messages and guidance in other ways.

The *emotional level* is the place where we create and release our emotions. It represents the emotions that are induced in the other three levels. Like the physical body, it is a repository for the other three. Instead of being a place where the imbalances show up, however, it is the place where the other three levels get to express themselves.

The *intellectual level* contains both what we think and how we think. It governs the thought patterns, perceptions and even the emotions that we have about certain ideas, concepts or events. If we get it into our thought process that something is sad, then when it happens we become sad because we have intellectually told ourselves that it will be so. Death can be one of these events. If you are brought up to believe that death is a sad event, than you will be sad when somebody dies. If you are brought up to believe that death is an event to be celebrated, then you will celebrate. However, there are certainly feelings associated with death that have nothing to do with thought processes-for instance, the feeling of loss. If your belief system is one in which you feel that a person is still around you, even when they are dead, then the feeling of loss might be less. But the physical absence of them in your life, depending on the role they played, will still bring up the feelings of loss. In some belief systems where death is seen as a reward for a good life, then the sadness might be that you have not earned your reward and that they have gone on to a better place. With this example, we have shown how thoughts can directly or indirectly lead to emotions. We have also shown how one's beliefs or perceptions can severely alter how and what different people might feel about the same experience.

As much as Western culture has prized the intellectual level throughout the last couple of hundred years, we have also made it both a weapon and a prisoner. As a culture we have tried to train it, toxify it and expand it but in only limited ways. As young children we are trained with what I call 'dog collar' terms. A dog collar term is one that is used to keep us 'in line.' We are threatened with eternity in hell, told what makes us good or bad, what is guaranteed to make us popular or desirable and what is sure to doom us to a life of crime or loneliness. The list goes on and on. We are taught who we must be to be happy, who to fear, who to love and even who to hate. This then shapes not only our perception of the world, but also our perceptions of ourselves. In our childhood, we can very easily have our own intellectual level turned against us. If done so in some specific ways, it will create a lifetime of misery and self-abuse. The teaching can come not only through what is said to us, but also what is role modeled in front of us. Our intellectual level is where our belief systems reside. Our intellectual level is often pitted against our physical level, our emotional level and our spiritual level. This leads to lives filled with physical problems, emotional pain and little or no spiritual connection.

Finally, we come to the *spiritual level*. Some call it soul. For others, it is a temple or the place of home—a home within ourselves. Our spiritual level is a hotbed of communication. Within it, we access our personal connection to the Divine and our connection to our own divine. It is within this level that one may talk with their higher self and/or another's higher self. It is here that we discover God/Goddess and the God/Goddess within. Here we also may access information, feelings and sensations that are beyond our physical body. It is also within this level that we may get information concerning the state and needs of our physical level, emotional level and intellectual level; as well as the state of these three levels in other people. It is also within the

spiritual level that we heal ourselves, help others to heal themselves and offer healing to all other things in which Divine is
contained. We are talking about all other living creatures, plants,
animals and the Earth itself.

As I proceed through the book and the levels, I will
expand on this information. I will also break the information on
the levels into sections. First, what was that level designed to do?
In the case of the physical level, I will be referring to our body
and the physical world as they exist today. Remember that not
only has our physical world been changing, but the body has been
evolving and changing as well. Most times the changes are slow
and only show up when you compare what we know of our
species a hundred or two hundred years ago and now. But beside
time as an indicator of change, we also have numbers. When
enough people are showing a certain quality or condition, we can
no longer ignore it. What I would like to make clear here is that
when I refer to something as being 'normal', I am not talking
about it in the context of normal versus abnormal. Today's usage
of the word normal is often an indicator of a good or bad reality
rather than an indication of something being different than what
we have previously experienced. We have a habit of only supporting or celebrating difference after it has somehow proven itself as
something culturally desirable. The way that we use normal in our
common context today is often an indicator of the concept of
'bad versus good.' For that context, I have developed this definition: *normalcy* is a social disease that, if left untreated, will most
likely prove fatal.

Second, after discussing what the level has been designed
to do, I will then discuss how we as a culture or society manipulate
our perception of how to appropriately '*be*' in that level. In many
ways, what I am looking at here is the kind of box to which the
level has been consigned. This is important because you need to
look at not only how the A.D.D. is affecting the person, but also
how our own cultural beliefs and mores play into the process. In
some cases, these beliefs and mores make the A.D.D. issue more
intense and more difficult than it actually is. It is important for
the A.D.D. person to understand the difference between the play

out of the A.D.D. and what problems they may be having as a result of cultural or social problems. These types of problems can cause difficulties for everybody, not just the person with A.D.D. It is vital to understand that many problems created around the person with A.D.D. are not about A.D.D. at all.

Third, I will discuss how the A.D.D. works within each level. The A.D.D. effect is not a simple one. In the work that I have done, the effects vary from a little to a great deal and have different expressions within a single level. In this section, under each level, I will explore the different patterns I have seen within that level and how they vary from person to person.

Fourth, I will discuss how to best utilize and manage those effects. In this section, I will examine some of the specific recommendations I have given clients to help with the A.D.D. effect. I will share things I have come across, as well as some of the things I have heard which make sense. In addition, I will share the successful things my clients have already developed to help them work with the effects.

Lastly, I will discuss how and why A.D.D. is a gift and a vital part of our evolutionary process. I will keep repeating that one of the earliest pieces of information I received concerning A.D.D. was the fact that it is a gift. It is part of the evolution of the species and an expansion of the human consciousness. We are 'medicating' our future away because it is easier than stretching our comfort zones and learning how to nurture and develop that future.

If you think about the permutations that are possible because of the variances of behavior within each level and between each level, it is easy to understand why A.D.D. can and does look so different from person to person. You may begin to understand why there are such wide variances of behaviors in people who are diagnosed with A.D.D. Think about the possible permutations when you have four different levels affected instead of one! One of the pieces of intuitive information that I have received while doing this work is that females are no less affected with A.D.D. than males, but they are affected differently. Because females tend to be less likely to have the more obvious responses in the physical level, it is easier to miss them. These facts, coupled with the way in which females are still socialized and prioritized, also adds to the factor of their A.D.D. being ignored. I also suspect that there are people who are going undiagnosed with A.D.D. because either they attend private schools, and/or are least affected in their physical level and/or have families that are more supportive of differences. Of course, I suspect that the number of people who are not diagnosed is lower than the number of children who are being misdiagnosed.

One of things to remember is that the levels are entwined and will affect each other. In other words, something that triggers an effect in one level might cause one of the other levels to react, depending on the intensity of what has happened. It is important to distinguish the source of the problem in order to help mediate it. After I have reviewed the levels completely, I will go into more depth about how these interactions might occur and what to do about them.

At this point you may feel that this book has already stretched your comfort zones farther than you are comfortable. All I can say is, stay open minded. The information that follows in the next several chapters has resonated in some form for every A.D.D. person, parent or spouse with whom I have worked. Even if you are not sure of what I have said so far, or even if you disagree with some of it, you can still benefit from what follows. If you have a desire to maximize your potential, to fully claim your uniqueness and to utilize your full brilliance, then read on. This may be the only book out there that tells you and constantly reminds you that *A.D.D. is a gift.*

Chapter 2
Physical Level

Before I break into the sections outlined in the first chapter, I would like to make one additional point concerning the physical level. Many people have felt it necessary to separate A.D.D. from A.D.H.D. (Attention Deficit Hyperactivity Disorder), but in my work I do not see that as necessary. This delineation breaks the A.D.D. effect on the physical level into two parts, but they still come from the same evolutionary process. Certain circumstances and outside influence might push a person from an A.D.D. to an A.D.H.D. diagnosis in the eyes of the medical world, but from my perspective these two diagnoses are the same issue. The two might often have slightly different needs or approaches. With A.D.H.D. for instance, things like diet, food sensitivities and allergies warrant more attention. Nevertheless, the two diagnoses tend to have more similarities than differences.

The Physical Body:
What has it been designed to do?

Though I look at the physical level as both the physical body and the physical world, for this section we will look at the physical body. In many ways, the physical body is like a processing plant. It is what we see, what we can touch and what can literally stop us in our tracks. It is our first line of defense in the world, the repository for all the unresolved imbalances of our other three levels. We have always idolized the physical body in one way or another. The specific physical characteristics that society idolizes in both genders has changed over time, but what has remained consistent is the fact that society does not promote or support individuality. Oftentimes, individually or as a group, we penalize those who are different even when those differences are ones over which the individual has no control. The challenge throughout the new millenium will be to avoid trying to genetically make everyone into someone else's idea of 'perfect.' Each person's idea of perfect is subjective and has no connection to any universal truth or reality.

The body mirrors our evolutionary path. We have become taller and less animal-like in our appearance and actions. We make fewer adjustments to seasons and shifts in temperature and have conditioned our bodies to be more accepting of foods and drinks from other cultures and other climates. The body has followed humanity's road of making the world a smaller place. Still other adjustments that have happened to the body are not visible to the naked eye. One of those adjustments is the movement towards less density. We have the ability to become lighter beings if we will allow ourselves. Our life span is extending and we no longer need to be as grounded or attached to the earth. This shift is certainly having its backlash. On one hand, we are lengthening life spans through better, lighter eating habits and decreasing our abusive habits. On the other, we struggle with addictions to drugs, alcohol and excesses—especially of comfort food and quick fixes. Our struggle comes out of the physical, emotional, mental and spiritual pain created by a society which denies us our uniqueness. We struggle with this change more than some evolutionary changes, not because it is coming too quickly, but because we have become resistant to change in areas that are not completely broken or which have not stopped working. We are also resistant to change that does not make our life easier. We have become a lazy culture, often looking for quick fixes.

Let us investigate how the body feeds itself energetically. Although the physical body obviously has a physical component, it also has an energetic component because it is one of the four *energy* bodies. The physical body receives energy in three ways.

The *first* way the body gets energy is through creating its own energy in the process of taking care of itself: eating, sleeping, exercising and breathing, to name a few. A body that is kept healthy, feeds itself well and exercises produces both the physical and the energetic fuel to maintain itself. In fact, even someone who eats unhealthy, does little or no exercise and manages to keep breathing produces some energy.

The *second* way in which the physical body can receive energy is from other people. Sometimes, with symbiotic energy exchange, energy will go to a place where synergy occurs. In other words, the sum is greater than the amount of its parts: synergy. You may feel or see this when two people are extremely engaged in a conversation, perhaps discussing something about which they are passionate. The conversation, the passion, takes on a life of its own and supercedes the energy of the participants. The other way in which energy is received from another can either be because it was given or because it was taken. Consciously or unconsciously, there are many people who create situations in which they either manipulate someone into giving them energy or they suck energy from the other person. They may also create a situation where an excess amount of energy is released and they 'feed' off it. Again, remember that some people do these things completely unconsciously. In his book *Invisible Armor: Protecting Your Personal Energy*, Thomas A. Hensel discusses these issues in detail.[1]

The *third* way to get energy is from a Divine source. This can be either directly or through an intermediary, as in the case of someone who does energy work which channels Divine energy. Sometimes the source of Divine energy can be either from the

---

[1] Hensel, Thomas A. *Invisible Armor: Protecting Your Personal Energy*. Portsmouth, NH: LightLines Publishing, 2000.

Divine directly or from your own higher self.

Now that we know how our physical bodies receive energy, what does our body do with it? There are a few obvious, biological processes such as general functioning and cell reproduction, but the physical body also uses energy to keep the emotional, mental and the spiritual levels working and (hopefully) healthy. Our physical body runs on what is most easily described as electrical currents. As this energy pours in and through our body, it creates a set of currents that then keeps the other currents going. There seems to be a maximum efficiency range where the least amount of input creates the maximum amount of output because of the efficiency of the vehicle conducting it. There is also a range of energy that we have found excessive. The excessive energy has often been associated with additional releases of adrenaline in the system, giving the body more energy than it can actually use at a given moment. This often results in something referred to as 'fight or flight' mode, in which a situation creates a reality that feels like a life or death situation. This rush of energy is then created so that the person can either fight or flee. Once the stimulation that created the situation is no longer valid, the body will release the excess energy. It is not unusual for the body to then go into an exhausted or depressive mode in order to recover.

Some things that we put into our body will create 'artificial energy,' which uses our life force energies. This artificial energy can create wear and tear if used in large enough dosages and, over prolonged periods, wear down our immune system. Some of the things that create artificial energy include drugs, caffeine, nicotine and some kinds of sugars; often things we associate with 'empty calories.'

Energy typically flows in rhythms. Every person has a natural rhythm. Just like some people are morning people, others are night people. Added on top of this natural rhythm are the rhythms created by our sleep habits and patterns, our food intake (both when we eat and what kinds of food we eat), and any physical and/or spiritual practices. If you follow your natural rhythms, fitting in the external factors harmoniously, you will consistently be working at peak performance. Your energy will then flow through you in a gentle pattern of building, peaking and resting.

The wonderful machine, our physical body, has put up with many abusive relationships, yet it seems to keep on ticking. Eventually, however, these habits will always take their toll. Some people have genetically received bodies that are better able to handle the abuses and keep on going. Others tend to be more sensitive and can tolerate less abuse.

The Physical Body:
The box we have created for it

As I mentioned earlier, we have put a great deal of pressure on fitting in and looking a certain way, even if we have to be self-abusive to achieve that 'ideal' look. We have also tried to assembly line the physical level in more ways than physical appearance. Each body has certain basic similar needs to other bodies, but these similarities are fewer than we have been led to believe. Each level has its own rhythm. What we have created in today's world is not only a lack of respect or support for these different rhythms, but also a number of artificial ways to meet the outside demands and expectations for physical performance. We are conditioned to abuse our physical body on a daily basis, to push it too much, to drug it to create additional performance and to ignore most, if not all, of our personal needs other than the most basic ones.

I want to examine what happens when we put together the concept of rhythms with the pre-existing concepts in both the traditional educational system and the workplace-obviously an 'oil and water' mixture. What we have been taught to prize is 'control,' in this case, control over the physical body. We prize it, we praise it and we punish those who do not have it even when it is beyond their control.

Let me share another story with you, a simple analogy about control. One of the children with whom I am working has a teacher who thinks the child urinates too often. Consequently, the teacher will usually deny the child's request to go the bath-room. This particular teacher sometimes had my client for a double period and would let other children go but would make this child wait because, in the words of the teacher, " He needs to develop more control."

Besides the ethical factors that that could easily be considered abusive and cruel, this type of situation could also lead to bladder infections. Control is not always a good thing. Our prizing of it often leads us to worry more about the efficiency of the individual rather than what is in their best interest. There is a correlation between the interruption of the body's natural flow and both short and long-term damage to that body.

Throughout our lives we are also given physical stereotypes and computer-generated prototypes that are impossible to achieve; teaching us that our body or appearance is lacking. We are directed towards a self-assessment which focuses on what we perceive or have been told is 'negative' or 'wrong' about the kind of physical body/looks that we have. This builds a reality that creates self-hatred for our body and directs negative energy towards ourselves, our body type, our looks or any other aspect of ourselves which does not measure up to the stereotypes. The same false realities exist around the life we live, the relationships we have, our desires and our dreams. We keep comparing ourselves to some false reality of perfection and failing.

We are taught to ignore the body's natural rhythms and replace them with artificial ones. We are not taught how to understand, utilize and find joy in our unique body. These are principles that effect everyone, but let us examine how the A.D.D. person is particularly affected.

The Physical Body: The A.D.D. impact

The A.D.D. impact on the body falls into the following categories: *processing energy sources, energy flows* and *energy reactions.* These are the areas most affected in the physical body of a person with A.D.D.

Processing energy sources

Earlier, we discussed the ways in which we receive the energy for the body's functioning. One was through a connection of Divine energy. The second was from either an exchange of or the taking of another person's energy and the third was the creation of energy through the consumption of caloric sources, sleeping and exercise. Here we look at the impact A.D.D. has on our relationship with the consumption of food and the overall maintenance of our body in processing that food.

When I began doing ADD work, this series of dietary information was the last of three pieces to fall in place around the physical body. The A.D.D. impacted person has a much higher tendency towards food sensitivities and tolerance issues with what they put into their body. Their body needs less to do more and has a lower tolerance to things that are going to clog up or slow the natural workings of the body. There are some foods, which seem to come up frequently, as problem foods. Problems foods fall into two categories: none or light. None is clear. Light however can fall into two additional categories: occasional or daily.

Occasional means these foods can be eaten occasionally with no adverse reaction. Daily indicates food that can be eaten daily but can not be eaten in large quantities. Whether light or none the kind of reactions that I detect can be anything from the exacerbating the acting out or energy rushes associated with A.D.D. to outburst of emotions. Though sensitivities vary from person to person, the following is a list of things for which a recommendation of a lighter diet has consistently appeared in my work:

Dairy	Artificial Flavorings
Wheat	Acidic Foods
Processed foods	Food Dyes
Processed sugars	Hydrogenated Oils

Again, I am not saying that every person who is impacted needs to cut all these things out of their diet. Try cutting back one of these things at a time and see if you notice a difference. Be aware of your diet and be willing to modify it.

This is not to say that every person who is impacted by A.D.D. has any or all of these sensitivities. I will say, however, that the people who have worked with me and who have been willing to become more aware and modify their diet have felt a positive difference. Diet is not the miracle answer. It is part of a protocol that can help the person. There are no wonder drugs, either prescription or alternative.

In the A.D.D. impacted body, there is also an increased sensitivity to drugs. This includes alcohol, caffeine, over-the-counter and prescription drugs. Like the food list, this does not mean, "no, never again, not all, do not even think about it." It simply indicates a need for awareness around what you are putting in your body. In the case of something like over-the-counter drugs, you may want to start with less than the recommended dosage.

Let's look at an example of how this might work out. Jenny was a third year college student. Jenny knew that she no longer wanted to be on Ritalin, but she worried about the fact that she had three more years before she would have the degrees she needed for her chosen field. After doing a scan, I found (among other things) that she had sensitivities to dairy, processed foods and sugars, alcohol, over-the-counter drugs (OTC) and coffee. Now, if you compare this to the earlier list you will see there were things that Jenny did not have sensitivity to, such as wheat. Her impact, like Jenny herself, is individual. First, I worked with Jenny to develop skills to help her with her schoolwork. After these were in place, we began to look at her diet and her eating habits.

When she and her mother decided that she should stop taking the Ritalin at the end of her school semester, her food cravings and caloric intake went up remarkably. This is not uncommon, as a common side effect of Ritalin can be loss of appetite. But she started putting on weight. After cutting back on the foods to which she was showing the sensitivities, she started eating even more of everything else. In working with her, I found two interesting things. One of the hardest things for her to give up was milk. She drank between one and two quarts a day. In addition, she was craving foods that had false energy attached to them, empty calories. When the three of us sat down again we agreed to have her focus on foods that were very nutrient dense as well as, some nutrient dense supplements in order to see if her eating would naturally stabilize. Her cravings decreased, she began to eat less, her weight began to go back to normal and her energy level was less erratic. She still had a high energy level, but it was more manageable and less hyper.

Energy flows

To explain the impact of A.D.D. on the energy flows of the body, I am going to use a voltage concept. It is important to understand that I am creating a scale for a comparison process that does not correlate with the actual volts as you experience them in the local electrical outlet. We will use the following scale: the typical person runs on 80-100 volts. If they are sick or run-down or just plain exhausted, they might be running on 70-80 volts. In a coma, they would have at least 50 volts going in order to sustain life functions, even if those functions were artificially supplied. In an extreme 'fight or flight', situation the person might may go up to 150 volts. During those rare cases where someone has performed a miraculous feat of strength, they may have soared up to 240. The 240 only lasts briefly, however, otherwise damage starts happening to the body. There would be a little more time tolerance for the 150, but it could not be maintained because we are just not wired for a steady current that large to go through our system.

A fit person who takes very good care of themselves and honors their rhythms might actually be able, through maintenance, to travel regularly at 100-110. This is that dynamic, high-energy person who always seems to be on the go without artificial energetic stimuli. The person who creates the energy through artificial means is the primary candidate for early heart attack or stroke. Because we are all individuals, we do have a hereditary factor that also influences us. Just as some people have a tendency to be more athletic, taller, have a faster metabolism or have better use of their psychic abilities, some people conduct their energy better. The A.D.D. impact affects energy in such a way that it travels in different patterns, generally at a higher base level. The patterns that I have either seen or received information about I will call *Steady*, *Pulse*, *Burst* and *Crescendo*.

Steady

The *Steady* pattern is evident in someone who typically runs 120-130 volts, a higher voltage than the 'typical' person accepted by society. These people most likely take good care of themselves. Depending on environmental support, diet and how the other three levels are being affected, these people are less likely to show up as A.D.D. They may look more like a type 'A' personality: high energy, tendency to be a workaholic, hard on themselves and very driven. As in all cases, diet, self-esteem, depression and other factors play into how this may look. Those factors may help suppress the energy level so that it fits in or might even be a little but lower, but this is not the person who is going to end up on the A.D.H.D. list. If there are emotional, medical or intellectual patterns in place which keep the energy suppressed, however, this person may have explosions of energy or a need to act out. In other words, if the pressure builds enough then the cork will pop.

Bobby, who we spoke about in the introduction, had a steady pulse with occasional bursts. Getting him involved with sports was a good idea. We also arranged his schedule so that he never had to go through more than two periods in a row at school without a period where he could let off excess energy, thus helping him maintain focus when in class. It is best if this child is allowed to go out and do something physical during study halls. If he attends too many classes in a row without some release, then he will have a forced burst from trying to hold back his extra, built-up energy.

Pulse

The *Pulse* pattern is one in which the energy may travel at either a high/normal or high/low energy pattern and have a regular flow of energy build and release in small waves. The variance is not going to be great, but will show up more likely as fidgeting, jerking or sudden needs to move or be doing something. This would look like someone with high energy or the person who we think has had too much sugar or caffeine. We might consider them slightly annoying, depending on the restrictions of the situation, but they can settle down if something interesting captures their attention. All the same factors as those that affect the person with the *Steady* energy pattern will also affect this person. The major difference is that the *Pulse* pattern has more of a rhythm to the energy. Once the rhythm has been identified, the person can be coached and trained to support the rhythm. With the *Pulse* pattern, one of the dangers or side effects is the higher energy base. If the energy base is around 125–150, then the person might try to consciously suppress the energy into more acceptable or less noticeable patterns. The person constantly attempts to suppress the 'unacceptable' energy with their own personal energy, creating an energetic version of grinding the gears. They may end up wearing themselves out, causing an increased need for sleep and even some potential long-term damage to their bodies.

Now let's introduce Mark, an eleven-year-old client. Mark has a pulse pattern of 135. So, envision an energy flow that peaks out at 135. Though Mark might be considered borderline hyperactive, he appears as if he constantly needs to be doing things. He reaches points where you would start to think he is hyperactive but then it seems to mediate and you think someone must have slipped him too much candy. Ideally, Mark should always have something to fidget with in his hands. He should get breaks between each concept that you are going over with him. When possible, I walk and talk with Mark when he is having a hard time understanding something and his energy pattern will help him grasp the concept.

Burst

The person with the *Burst* pattern goes along calmly for a time, followed by a sudden burst of energy which is similar to a fight or flight kind of release, perhaps even up to that miracle level of energy. These bursts tend to be in a pattern that is often predictable or at least discernable. My sense tells me that working with one of these individuals over a longer period and eliminating the outside factors would make the pattern more evident. The frequency and intensity of the bursts can be affected by diet, anxiety and outside pressure. The outside pressure can be defined as how much and for how long they must mediate their energy or are being forced to do so. The non-burst energy may run either normal or high.

If this person runs at 120 volts but is trying to keep it at 90 because this is what the situation is demanding, when a burst does come, it might be a 240 instead of 180. The fact of the matter is that this energy comes in and must go somewhere. This pattern is much less likely to be affected by depression or low self-esteem. The reason that this is true is that, from an energetic perspective, there is a cleansing effect about a burst. It is like a good windstorm that stirs everything up but leaves the place clean when it is over.

Now let's meet Justin aged twelve years. Justin's pattern is usually 132, but he has bursts of 176 to 212. Justin is the kind of child who is into everything, very curious and very energetic. He can also be very self-aware and can keep himself occupied as long as he has strong structures and rules. Occasionally, he will have these bursts when he is not allowed to regularly work out the energy that travels through him. In his case, as often happens in people with burst patterns, poor diet, anxiety or emotional releases will trigger the burst. So, when Justin bursts you need to first let him run around and expend as much energy as he needs to become calm again. Then check in with him and see what triggered him. Enforced confinement, foods to which he is sensitive or emotional releases will be consistent triggers.

Crescendo

As you might think from the title, this is the energy style that builds to the point of a major energetic release. It tends to run in pattern forms like the pulses, but instead of staying in a small wave pattern, they build to a tidal wave, crash and then start all over again. Though you may perceive the crash as a bad thing, it is not. The crash does not have to be a violent or dramatic. In fact, it might look like a nap, reading a book or watching some television. The *Crescendo* pattern may have mini-pulse patterns as part of it, but instead of the patterns staying within a regular pulse, they shift and grow each time. So, it may start as a pulse of 135-145, then shift to 140-150 or it may start 135-145 then jump up to 145-155(which creates a different looking pattern). These patterns, if at all influenced, will be more influenced at the earlier levels by the some of the same things that influence a pulse pattern. However, as the energy gains momentum, the patterns will be less affected. For someone who is medicated or depressed, there will be a punch-through point where neither medication nor depression is a factor anymore. In fact, that punch-through point will be like an energy rush.

We are going back to Jenny, the third year college student. She had a *Crescendo* pattern and, because of her mother's involvement, we could correlate it to body rhythms. We created a schedule during her day where she would do her studying when her rhythms were lower and physical activities when they were higher or at their highest. Diet, sleep patterns and times as well as outside pressures could shift how a pattern might build or play out. These things could even get it to kick off so that it matched the rhythms for her class schedule.

All these patterns have their own rhythm and timing. Only when you can separate the timing and the rhythm from the outside factors can you work effectively with them. Oftentimes, when I work with an older child or a young adult where the parent is involved, the parent will recognize the pattern. When I explain what this would look like. That is often because it was easier to see when the child was younger- especially before the child started taking medication or eating poorly. To me, this is not an indicator that the pattern goes away with age. It probably means that the more outside pressure and interference become involved the more likely it is that the pattern will be masked. Adults who have had a medicated and/or traumatic life are less likely to recognize the pattern immediately. In addition, more and more people suspect, myself included, that alcoholism, drug addiction and other kinds of addictions might have a correlation with A.D.D.

The Physical Body: Managing The Gift

As you may have already figured out, what adjustments or schedules you create depend on what types of energy flows you have. For all the energies, you should start by looking at these issues: diet, what is being asked of the A.D.D. impacted person and what is being role modeled to them. Next, for all the energies you should look at creating physical breaks that will allow the energy to dissipate as necessary. As rhythms are being discerned, schedule the day to support those rhythms. When something requires the person to hyperfocus, they must schedule some form of releasing time at regular intervals.

For *Steady* and *Pulse* patterns, the following protocols have been helpful: alternating activities, moving meditations, learning while doing something physical, kinesthetic learning and the use of video and audio tapes. Some of what will be most effective depends on the learning style of the individual and what kind of mental impact they have. The secret of managing the *Steady* and *Pulse* styles is to not let energy become suppressed for an extended period of time or force the rhythm to fight against itself. If either happens regularly, someone who does not have a burst pattern will have a forced, pressure-induced burst. This kind of burst is both counter-productive and harmful, particularly if it happens too often.

Burst and *Crescendo* patterns are best managed through creating regularly scheduled activities that release excess energy. The first thing, to remember with this pattern, is that it is a building pattern. This means that the amount of energy that goes through the person will become greater and greater. When a build is happening, it is best to coordinate activities to mirror the increasing energy. I put these two styles together because each will have a crash time after a release. The more intense the release, the more intense the crash. A burst might have a brief crash or what might even be perceived as a letdown. After a crash or letdown has occurred, the person will start to build energy again. This is the best time to do activities that take a focused and mental energy but not much physical energy. As time goes on and the person's energy continues to build, it is best to decrease the still activities and increase the more physical ones. One of the things to identify, in this pattern, is when the person has to hyperfocus, in order to pay attention to something. When a point of hyperfocus is reached, it is time to start moving the activities from inactive to increasingly more physically active.

One of the things that can throw a monkey wrench into the self assessment process of what energy pattern you have is that someone with either *Burst* or *Crescendo* pattern can have the *Pulse* pattern as the base from which they start. In addition, someone with a *Burst* pattern could also have a *Steady* pattern as the base. It is not unusual for someone I am working with or someone who has come to one of my workshops to say that, while they resonate to either the *Steady* or *Pulse* pattern they do sometimes get bursts. What you need to examine at this point is the regularity of the bursts. If you have bursts on any kind of regular basis, then you probably have a crossover pattern. A crossover pattern would be someone who has elements of both patterns existing. If the bursts are occasional, then it may just be one of those pressure releases because you have been working too much against your pattern or have been suppressing too much energy too frequently.

Other factors seem to skew these patterns, including what is going on in your other levels that may feed or mediate the patterns.

Understand that I am simply trying to give you tools to assess something in yourself or a loved one. As far as specific recommendations, here are a few:

1) Plan and implement sedentary work projects so that after each one you get up and do something to help shake off excess energy.

2) If you need to do something, which is going to take a long period of time or intense focus and concentration, start by breaking it up into smaller pieces. If possible, take not only the energy release breaks, but also alternate the project pieces with working on something else.

3) While doing homework, break it up into equal time slots of 'on homework' and 'off homework.' Depending on the energy pattern and the mental impact, the time periods will change. Try 15 or 20 minutes on and then 15 or 20 minutes off and see how that works. Be willing to adjust.

4) Try to do some kind of physical release activity before any class or meeting.

5) Incorporate the following into your routines:

> *Breathing exercises*
> *Visualizations*
> *Diet modifications*
> *Moving meditations*
> *Regular exercise routines*
> *Energy work, either by you or by someone else.*
> *Supplement recommendations*
> *Keep objects handy with which you can fidget.*

Another thing which has been an interesting discovery is that certain kinds of games, like Nintendo, Game Boy, Sega, computer games and other such systems, will actually create simulated feelings of movement which allow energy to release.

Remember that not everyone with A.D.D. is going to be

affected in the physical body in a way that clearly stands out. Someone might be much more affected in the emotional, mental or spiritual level and only mildly affected on the physical level. The milder the effect, the easier it is for the person to mediate it. Unfortunately, mediating it might or might not be in a way which is healthy or in the best interest of the person. If I deal with someone who is A.D.D. and yet seems to have little or no physical characteristics of it, I always check and try to eliminate anything that may be mediating it in a negative way. It can then be managed and utilized in a healthy manner.

Anytime I do these scans and create protocols I always start with baby steps. Make little changes at first and let them settle in before making more changes. Recently, I met with a mother and teenage child and when I did the scan, the list of this child's food sensitivities became apparent. As soon as I finished, the mother immediately started telling the child "none of this, no more of that." I watched as the child shut down and I saw the beginnings of a battle that could easily end up as a war . . . a war where there are no winners, only losers. I took the mother out of the room and told her that we would address the food issues a little at a time. I also mentioned how important it was that the child willingly participate in the process in order to meet their goal of no medication. It works well this way. If the child participates and you introduce gradual changes, you do not have to worry about the 'binge behind your back' eating or any other kind of self-sabotaging due to resentment. So take a tip from me: if you are going to try any of these things, do them gently and slowly at first.

The Physical Body:
Why the A.D.D. Impact is a gift

Once they understand their particular energy flow and rhythm, the A.D.D. impacted person has the ability to get more done. This leaves more time to do what want to do instead of what they need to do, and they will be able to do it in the most efficient manner. Their body will become more able to handle more energy with less wear and tear.

Food intolerance and sensitivities exist to help us keep ourselves away from those things that are not good for us either in larger quantities or sometimes in any amount. Someone with these kind of patterns may only sleep every day and half and need no more sleep than that, as long as they are awake and functioning. This is due to their energy flow and not because of an artificially created awakeness. These people can better create energy for themselves. They will bring more energy into exchanges with others, have no reason to take others' energy and they will be able to hold more Divine energy.

One of the best analogies that I could come up with is that this new way of energy is like the switch from oil or gas to solar power. It is a much less limited force that is more earth friendly and more efficient, once you know how to use it.

Summary For The Physical Body

So, what does the A.D.D. impacted person need to remember about the physical body? To start, keep in mind that the pre-A.D.D. body was developed in a time when food sources were plentiful, natural and nutrient dense. Humans were much more connected to the energies and the rhythms of both the planet and everything on the planet. This new evolving body is designed to react against artificial, toxified foods with little or no nutritional value. It will not work well eating what is quick and available. This body is becoming increasingly resistant to putting large quantities of chemicals into it. It is creating survival mechanisms through reactions to certain foods, drugs and chemicals. In addition, this body is designed to do more with less because we have less 'quality' left in the foods that are available; so the body needs to find things that are nutrient rich.

This body also demands that if you are going to use it properly you are going to have to discover and work within its rhythms. By doing so, you can become more efficient, with less stress and with no need for false energy sources.

Have you ever noticed the more efficient and progressive technology becomes, the more we need to take care of it correctly? Look at this body as the newest in technology. We are still figuring it out and we need to treat it gently, but the future is looking pretty good.

Chapter 3
Emotional Level

Of the four levels, the emotional level is the most affected by the impact of A.D.D. This level has become increasingly limited and misconstrued; it has been diverted from the job it is supposed to perform. It is possible that the emotional impact is greatest because we have been trained to separate ourselves from our emotions. As my work with A.D.D. began to unfold, I had difficulty determining why its impact is a gift within the emotional level. Once the answer was given, it seemed so simple. It works that way sometimes. In order for me to share the answer with you, however, we must understand not only what the emotional level was designed to do, but also how dysfunctional we have made it. I will discuss the dysfunctional way we deal with this level as well as the subsequent results. Then I will spend time on how to rectify these things. If the people around the person with A.D.D. cannot role model and support healthy emotions, then this severely limits the possibility of the A.D.D. person coming to grips with their emotional level.

The Emotional Level:
What has it been designed to do?

The emotional level is the place where the energies that become our emotions are created as well as the place where these emotions are held. It is also an integral part of our memories. The most powerful of these are sensate-based. These types of memories are strongest and clearest when associated with something we saw, smelled, touched and, most powerfully, felt at that moment. We are sensate beings. Feelings are sensate; emotions are feelings.

Emotions themselves are simply energy in motion. Energy in MOTION becomes EMOTION. For most people, the event or thought occurs, energy is created and then that energy goes into motion. This energy is created as a response or a reaction to some outside stimuli—perhaps an event, an experience or an interaction. We might have been told something, felt something, seen something or all the above. The emotion that is released might give us insight to a thought pattern or perception that we have. It might indicate a message from the physical level. It could be a message from the Divine or even our higher self. It might stir a memory we need to look at or issue we need to resolve. There are many possibilities. Remember that the emotional level is a repository for the other three levels as well as a support system, a reminder and a communications link. It is the bridge between each of the other three levels and our conscious mind as well as a link between the conscious and the unconscious.

The emotional level was designed to be the place that holds our passions. We derive our motivation from this level. Creativity can reach transcendence from this place. Great works of art are born, pictures are painted, music is written, music is played, poetry is created, books are born, plays are performed and songs are sung from this place. This level most separates us from the other species with which we share the planet. Our ability for complex emotions creates this separation and it is the passion drawn from our emotional level that drives us to better ourselves as a species.

In many Eastern philosophies, emotions are associated with certain organs or other parts of the body. Some spiritual and healing systems indicate that certain organs or parts of the body will even hold unresolved emotions and that imbalances within the body indicate unreleased emotions. For example, we often associate the emotion of love with the heart. We refer to someone, as 'dying of a broken heart' if they had a great emotional trauma, became ill and died. You and I both know that if we open that person's chest cavity, the heart would not be broken . . . but the metaphor remains.

The Emotional Level: The box we have created for it

Now, let us look at what we as a culture have done with and to the emotional level. Emotions are often considered handicaps. We are taught, either through direct teachings or through role modeling, that emotions are a weakness. The reason we must understand emotions and what they look like when they are healthy is so that we can help the impacted person sort what problems are related to the A.D.D. impact and what part has to do with cultural and family dysfunction about emotions.

We have also done emotions the disservice of classifying them according to gender. Women are discounted because of emotions and men are told that they are less manly if they have emotions on a regular basis. A male is allowed (and expected) to have certain emotions as long as they are controlled, appropriate and infrequent, but females are judged, often unfairly, by the expression of their emotions. We do not have many good role models of either sex to show our children that emotions are good, healthy and necessary in order to be in balance. We are taught to judge our emotions and to judge ourselves because of the emotions we either feel or express. We are taught to keep our emotions inside and are forced to pretend to either not have them or to control them. At that point, the repressed emotions either eat us from the inside out or they come out in explosive ways. The pressure will erupt eventually— if it does not kill us first.

People get into trouble when either they shove emotions back down and refuse to let them out or try to 'intellectualize' them and pretend that they are controllable. Emotions are often released in inappropriate ways; frequently in ways that do not truly dissipate what the real energy was about. This might play out as overreacting to a situation (either good or bad) and/or becoming violent or abusive. It can be those unreleased or unexpressed emotions that lead to physical imbalances.

The control of emotions has been role modeled to us as a form of strength—a sign of discipline and even courage. This is utterly ridiculous. It is much more courageous, disciplined and strong to have your emotions and do to so in a centered way. But what we are shown is a picture of no emotions, tightly controlled emotions or explosive emotions. The first two are a sign of fear that having the emotion is going to make you lose control. The last one is typical of someone who is either being reactionary because they are out of control or they have shoved so many unresolved or unreleased emotions down that these emotions have erupted and the person experienced what I call emotional vomiting.

Control… reaction… suppression. It is time to elaborate on these concepts. We need to discuss why we often do not understand them. Examine why we use them to abuse ourselves with. First, there are only two things we can control and any other kinds of control we think we might have are illusion— illusion we cling to because they give us a feeling of safety. But even this feeling of safety is an illusion. If you do not think control is an illusion, then stop for a moment and put yourself in the bombed Oklahoma City Federal Building. How much control did they have? See yourself in Christopher Reeve's place on that last day he ever rode a horse. Was there any control there? How about being the parent of a child who was born with a terminal illness? Are you in control? Or the person whose beloved spouse died in an automobile accident? Where is your control? There are only two things we *can* control: whether we choose to respond or react in any given situation and the actions we choose to take.

Reaction or response? You choose. What is the difference? A big one. When we are involved in a situation and we feel the emotions start to rise, that is when we get to choose. Response is going into that place of center, touching what the feelings are, understanding them and then replying accordingly. You have sorted out what was said or done that needs a reply. You also have to sort out what has nothing to do with what has just happened and what part of the situation is attached to another issue, another time or another person. It could even be an issue you have with yourself. But when you reply, you are replying to what was said or done in the moment and you reply from a place of your center. Do not get me wrong. Of course, you maybe angry, be hurt, frustrated or any other number of emotions. This simply means that you are having the emotions that are specifically attached to the situation or person. When the experience is over, you can then go back and see what other actions need to be taken or what other issues need to be resolved.

A reaction is just that: the act of 'acting back.' It is a defensive maneuver where you feel as though someone is taking an action against you and so you act back, or 're-act.' Reaction is a place of giving your power to the other person, situation or experience. Some people, when they feel like they are going to be in a place of reaction over something, decide the best way to deal with it is to act first. That is equally counter-productive to the process. At the very least, it is counter-productive to the process of successful communication, resolving issues, and/or the winning of friends and influencing of people.

We, as a society, are afraid of losing control to emotions. Or perhaps we do not like how they make us feel. We are often unsure what to do with them. If no role modeling has occurred on how to deal with emotions, then we definitely venture into scary territory when we have them. Therefore, the next logical step is to say to ourselves, "Let's just not have them." Unfortunately, even separating ourselves from our emotional level (more common than you think) does not stop the process. In the nanosecond that a little energy is created over something which has happened, that energy moves and emotion is born.

When we say to ourselves, "Well, if I cannot stop myself

from having the darn things, I won't let them out. Then I will not have to deal with them," suppression has been born. What happens when we suppress? Well, the energy is in motion so we literally force our body to contain it. It floats around, building up first in our emotional level. If we then leave it for too long a time or try to hold too many emotions, they get 'stored' in our physical body. Pressure builds and the energies begin what is usually a very slow process of synergy; a process where what is created is larger than the sum of its parts. The person will reach a point where there is so much built up energy that the energy must find a way to release itself. An unresolved or unexpressed emotion is like a festering wound. In this case, the emotional level becomes infected instead of the physical body, at least initially. In this case, anything that elicits the same emotions as those being repressed can create irrationality, within the individual. The more repression that there is, and the longer it stays repressed, the more synergy can occur. Which means the person can become completely irrational, explosive, even obsessive over the issues attached to that repression.

One way for someone to release these emotions is to erupt instead of channeling the emotion towards that which caused it. You find some catalyst to which you can overreact and then release some of the extra, built-up energy. We know this as 'letting off steam.' Unfortunately, misdirecting energy is like draining the puss from an infected wound. You can drain it all you want, but if you do not clear up the infection, the wound will not heal. The immediate effect is that the eruption will release pressure, which when it is too built up, can be harmful. In the end, however, the more you drain and refill the wound, the more permanent damage you will cause.

Another way to release suppressed emotions is to find a situation or person that you can take your aggression out on. Not all unexpressed emotions are painful or angry emotions. However, built-up pressure is built-up pressure regardless of the specific emotion. So, if you have loving emotions for someone who is not comfortable letting you express them, then you may be overly effusive to someone else you care about. Eventually it becomes uncomfortable and frustrating. Eventually the pressure makes you angry, adding yet another layer to the emotions. Anger is often the emotion we use to spearhead all the other emotions. Therefore, when someone has an explosion the emotions will often shoot out like an arrow, with anger being the arrowhead and the rest of the emotions being the feathers on the other side of the arrow. In other words, your unresolved emotions make you a bully. You find someone you have power over and release your frustration onto them. This may lead you to become abusive or a perpetrator.

The emotions may also tie together and try to release themselves through revenge. Unlike the previous example, the target of the revenge is someone who has contributed to at least some of the issues. Elder abuse is a good example, often an unconscious one. The adult child has unresolved and unexpressed emotions from their childhood. They were often raised in an environment where one or both parents shut down the open and honest communication of emotions. The child as an adult becomes a caretaker of that parent and suddenly starts treating that parent the way they, in their mind, perceived they were treated as a child. Now they have a parent who is the helpless child. They may even see nothing wrong with their behavior because they are being no different than their parents. In some cases that may be true. That does not make it appropriate, but it may be accurate. In other cases, however, thirty or forty years of suppressed emotions have a way of skewing the reality of what truly happened. The adult child may even be functioning from the emotional level of the actual child that they used to be. Their emotions can warp their reality.

Yet another way to release suppressed emotions is to become self-abusive or find someone to abuse you. You may become involved in abusive work situations, romances or friendships; and/or you may adopt self-abusive behaviors. You may smoke, or become one of the –holics: alcohol, work or food. Then there are always the addicts: drugs, abuse, sex or dependency. Most of these, if not all, lead back to unresolved emotions about issues from the past. And these emotions are not always unexpressed emotions relating to someone else. They may be negative emotions that you have about yourself. Of course, there is also the reality that life as a victim allows you to either victimize others through your victim status or receive a great deal of energy which is poured your way. You get support in the areas where you are being victimized, lapping up the energy like a cat does cream. You also get to avoid responsibility for your life and dodge the unresolved issues. Martyrs have been born from this cycle.

For example, when people come to me with an issue of trying to stop smoking, one of the first things that I do with them is find out what emotions were they trying to 'suck back down' inside of themselves when they started smoking. The habit of smoking literally aids us in containing our emotions. We inhale them into ourselves instead of expressing them. You will find most of the addictions find their roots in difficulty with the expression emotions. Smoking helps us swallow them, alcohol may either provide us the permission we feel we need to express our emotions or numb us to them. The same applies to drugs. Some drugs are just a release for pent-up emotions to create numbness that supports us in trying to separate from our emotional level.

The final way in which we process suppressed emotions is by keeping them inside. With these pent-up emotions beating away at our insides, we will eventually become sick or even die from trying to hold them down. We are becoming increasingly aware of how much our emotional health is related to illness. For example, depression literally depresses our immune system. Have you ever noticed that we refer to people in emotional trauma as being 'eaten up by their emotions'? And have we not heard, perhaps even said, that someone was 'eaten up by cancer'? Coincidence? Maybe. Maybe not.

These are some of the things that we have done to our poor emotional level. And these are also some of the things to keep in mind when I go over some of the protocols that I have established for people to help them manage their A.D.D.

The Emotional Level:
The A.D.D. Impact

The way in which the emotional level is changed by
A.D.D. is significant. We talked before about the fact that, when
something occurs, energy is created which then goes into motion
and becomes an emotion. When energy is created in a person
with A.D.D., however, it does not go into motion. It just sits there
as though contained by a holding tank. This happens in several
different ways. In each case, the energy is held and when enough
energies have been collected the emotions all release at the same
time—what I call a *drop*. Like the physical patterns discussed
earlier, the emotional patterns occur in a variety of manners and
rhythms. This pattern of holding and releasing energy (hold and
drop) creates a ball of emotions that suddenly rush through the
person's body. The person must then deal with many, different
emotions. A common result is the creation of one or two more
emotions, usually frustration and/or anger. Then the explosion
occurs. I have seen three primary variations of this pattern: *Hold
Drop, Squeeze Hold Drop* and *Hold Drop with Aftershock*.

<u>Hold Drop</u>

The *Hold Drop* pattern is simply one in which the energies,
the specific emotions, will hold until a certain number of emotions are reached they then drop and the person gets them all at
once. I have seen the numbers vary from *three* to *eighteen*. Herbert,
one of my first A.D.D. clients, was 62 years old. His *Hold Drop*
pattern was *three*. That meant that he would experience two
events that created emotions, which would go into the holding
tank until the third emotion hit. Then all three emotions would
release in one drop. Having three emotions at once might not
sound so bad, but they could be (at the very least) a bit confusing.
Herbert, however, was from that old school where men were not
supposed to show emotions. There were only certain emotions it
was acceptable to show. Because there were only three, he could

often do just as other had role modeled—shove them right down inside. Moreover, he could do this for three or four rounds of *Hold Drop* patterns until the drop would release a trigger so that all the rest of the 'shoved down' emotions erupted. This created an overload of emotions from both ends: his suppressed emotions and his emotional drops. Herbert spent most of his adult life as a rageaholic. When he started to accept the concept of dealing with the emotions, he improved. However, he would still have flare-ups. When he finally understood these concepts and started working with the protocol I outline at the end of this chapter, the intense rages became a thing of the past—as long as he continued to pay attention to his patterns.

Squeeze Hold Drop

The *Squeeze Hold Drop* pattern is one in which some small part of the energy goes into motion—maybe 10% to 15%. The person feels either nothing or only a little bit of energy. Then, when enough separate energies are held back, they will all drop into motion in a manner similar to the *Hold Drop* pattern. Jenny had a pattern of *thirteen* emotions. Unlike Herbert, who felt nothing until the drop, Jenny would know something was wrong. She would feel what I call the shadow of energy, but it usually would not get her full attention until she had a drop. After thirteen emotions were built-up in that holding tank, she would be walloped with a big ball of confused and disorienting emotions.

Hold Drop with Aftershock

The last pattern I have detected, the *Hold Drop with After-shock*, has been one that has more to do with rhythm than anything else has. In the first two patterns, a number seems to trigger the release. When identified, the releases fall into a rhythm or pattern. With the *Hold Drop with Aftershock* pattern, the initial number of held emotions seems to be higher maybe thirteen, fifteen or even eighteen. After this drop, however, there is a second drop after two, three or four more emotions have been held. The aftershock might be a single aftershock or a double aftershock. Mark had a drop pattern of 12-2-4, which meant that twelve events could occur and then there would be a drop. Then, as if the holding tank did not quite reset, itself, there would be a second drop after two more experiences. After that, it took four more emotions for another drop and then he returned to the original pattern of twelve. Does this sound confusing? When I explained it to his mother, she thought for a moment and confirmed it.

She saw it like this: "Mark would be fine for a while and then suddenly out of nowhere, he would have this emotional outburst, like a temper tantrum. Before he could really even get calmed down, he would get all upset again and then he would seem to start getting better and boom it would happen again. Then he would be fine for a while again. Both his father and I noticed it. And when all the explosions were said and done, most of the time he could not even tell us what had upset him. He did not want to talk about it. And he would seem fine."

This pattern creates a person who, most of the time, goes around with very light or no emotions. They then experience an explosion of emotions, which are very confusing. More than one of my clients has described that in-between period as monotone or flat. Then chaos. Exhaustion. Then flat again.

When I began communicating these findings to my clients, it was interesting to note that there was either complete acceptance of what I was seeing or complete denial about the flat or emotionless periods. At first I was confused, until one day when I was dealing with one of my adults with A.D.D. who had been diagnosed over ten years earlier. She had tried all the traditional routes and was on medication. She was also very good at what I called 'A.D.D. speak.' She knew all the pet phrases that had been developed by the traditional medical community, some of which said nothing. But they sounded good when explaining to someone why he or she had to be on medicine in order to be normal. After I explained the messages I had received about the *Hold Drop* patterns to her, our conversation went like this:

"That's what the doctors call impulsivity," she told me.
"And what does that mean?" I asked.
"It refers to impulsive emotional outbursts," she replied.
"Caused by what?" I asked her. "Or better yet, meaning what?"
"It means when you have all sorts of emotions come out at once."
"Why?" I wanted to know.
"Nobody knows, as far as I know," she informed me.
"So what does impulsivity tell you, beyond its description?"
"Nothing, I guess, but it sure does sound good, I think." She
looked at me quizzically.

As I worked with her more, trying to get her to understand about the emotional flat periods, I finally hit pay dirt.
Although she was struggling to understand them, she told me to
keep going because, as I was talking about these periods, it was
bringing up emotions for her. This was telling her that I was on
the right track. Although she did not fully understand, she knew I
was saying something that was true or she would not be having
these reactions. At that moment, something special was given to
me. I realized what was happening to these children with A.D.D.
They developed what I call an *intellectual-emotional level*. For them it
is a self-protection mechanism or survival skill; one they developed so young, they did not know it existed. It is a survival
mechanism because it makes them 'look' like everyone else who is
in their world. It feels safer.

To best explain the *intellectual-emotional level*, it would be
helpful to put things into a situational perspective. By the time
children are three years old, they are observing and figuring out
their place in the world. They are observing more than they have
the capacity to express. They can talk, but they are seeing things
they have not yet learned the words to describe. And they are
certainly experiencing realities that are beyond their capacity to
identify by more than the simplest of terms. They are learning
what kinds of actions bring positive responses and what kinds of
actions bring negative responses.

By four years of age, they have definitely begun to understand what is expected of them; not only by their parents, but also

by most of the people who are in their world. It is at around four or five, at the time they begin interacting with other children in larger groups, that they begin to fully understand what makes them like others and what makes them different. For that child with A.D.D., life is a very different place—especially in light of what is happening in the physical, intellectual and spiritual levels. Because of those impacts, they may be standing out in ways that are not being perceived as 'good.' The emotional level, however, is a completely different thing. This child is expected to have certain emotional responses. If they do not have them, then they are asked what is wrong with them.

Children are natural mimics. The child impacted with A.D.D. may see that they are supposed to be happy, sad or even upset about something when instead they feel nothing. Then some terrible ball of feeling is released and a drop has happens, often scaring them. Then they are seen as either overreacting or reacting inappropriately. Depending on the people around them and other factors in the environment, they may be asked questions for which they have no answers. They may be shouted at or threatened. The message to them is that they are not fitting in and that they are not understood by those people who represent their safety, their world. This is not a good thing.

So these children go into observer mode and begin to figure out how they are *supposed* to react to any given situation. Then, right on cue, they react that way. They may even receive positive responses or rewards because they are now acting like everyone else. People stop asking them, "Are you sick? What is wrong with you? Don't you like the present? Or the ride? Or the game?" Now they fit in. And when they do have the drops, they do their best to separate, hide or downplay them.

Often, this starts happening at the age of three, four or five. By the time that child reaches just seven or eight, they have done it so long and so often that it is now a part of them. Many of them do not even realize that this is something they have created. If they still remember, they really hide it now because, at this age, peer pressure is certainly becoming a factor. They are afraid if anyone ever finds out the truth of how terribly and drastically different they are, they will never be loved or accepted. They might even be thrown away. Adults with whom I deal usually struggle at first with the concept of the *intellectual-emotional level* because it is a great, deep, dark, painful secret to them. I would compare it to the abused child who has actually shut out a memory or created a behavior which they swear is 'just who they are' because of the potential danger in owning it for what it truly is.

In case you did not know, children are very sensitive to energy. They can feel other people's moods; they can feel concern, worry or disapproval. They know when their parents are not happy with them. They know when they are being singled out for the wrong reasons. I have two stories I would like to share to illustrate this. One concerns a teenager and the other an adult. Let us first discuss the teenager, a fifteen-year-old whom I will call Jonah. When I explained to Jonah about the emotional *Hold and Drop* pattern, he was very fascinated by the whole concept. I could see he was dissecting and applying the information as quickly as I was disseminating it. Jonah is a very intelligent, quick-minded and quick-witted young man with self-esteem issues due to his A.D.D.

As we talked, he referred to what he calls the 'flat' period. He could clearly see how these periods happen in his life, and the sudden emotional burst was a 'no brainer'. However, he struggled with the idea that he created an *intellectual-emotional level*. Suddenly, he looks at me and blurts out, "Christmas mornings."

"Okay, I'll bite. What about Christmas mornings?" I asked.

"As a small child I remember having no real response to the presents under the Christmas tree. And how my parents seemed disappointed. They kept asking me if I liked my gifts. I did. I even told them that I did, but they said I did not seem very happy. After a couple of Christmas mornings I started 'being happy and excited' and they weren't disappointed any more."

As we talked more, he then started to understand how he had created an intellectual-emotional level.

My second story involves one of the adults with whom I worked. We will call him Brian. He and I were discussing the flat periods and he recalled the following story:

"I was youngest of five children. Much younger. And I will always remember my fourth birthday party. My birthday is in December. And my parents did not want it to get lost to the holidays." He paused.

"And?" I queried.

"They threw me this birthday party at this ice cream shop. And I remember that it was fun and all the kids were having a really good time. But they all seemed really excited, almost hyper, like you would think a bunch of four-year-olds were at a birthday party, at an ice cream shop." He paused.

"I take it you weren't, hyper and excited, like everyone else?" I asked.

"No. Don't get me wrong, it was fun, but my response was definitely low. No jump-up-and-down-in-the-air-oh-boy-this-is-fun. They referred to me as a shy, bright, but subdued child, a lot."

"Did something else happen?"

"Yes, part of my surprise was they had hired a Santa Claus to come in and give me my birthday gifts. As soon as he came in and started toward me saying 'Ho, ho, ho,' it was like all these emotions exploded in me. I was completely overwhelmed. I started hysterically crying I threw myself on the floor, crawled under the table and would not come out or stop crying until he left. And it wasn't like by that point I did not know who Santa Claus was, it was just all the emotions that I felt which completely overwhelmed me. At that point I knew I was different than other kids."

"How did that affect you?"

"Well, I tended to stay very close to my mother. I always wanted her around. She was very good at letting me be a little adult. She never pried about how I was feeling. And if I felt one of those emotional things start to happen I learned to either shove it down or went someplace by myself where I could cry until the feelings went away. I avoided situations where I was expected to have emotions, and if I was in one, I learned to give them what they wanted."

"When did you figure out that you had created what I am calling an intellectual-emotional level?"

"When you explained to me what it was. I just figured out that the reason why Santa Claus sent me into hysterics was that him showing up must have created a drop. But at four, I just knew I was terrified and I could not explain. Now I know why I went into theater and why I always avoided emotions like they were my enemy unless I was on stage."

Do not confuse the *intellectual-emotional level* with intellectualizing emotions. They are very different. If it were role modeled to someone to shove down or intellectualize their emotions, then they may try to do that when they have a drop. However, if they have the kind of hold-drop pattern that is higher than three or four, it is nearly impossible. What they may do is become a rageaholic when a drop occurs, but when someone is intellectualizing their emotions they are shoving them back down and creating damage. With the A.D.D. impact, the person does not get to utilize the message or communication link that the emotional level was created to provide. So, if one or more of the emotions in a drop is a message, it is clearly being garbled in the midst of all the other messages. Therefore, the message is not being received.

So, let's review one last time the difference between intellectualizing the emotional body and an intellectual-emotional level. Intellectualizing the emotional body is telling yourself how you should feel about something even when you are feeling something different. It is like telling yourself that you should not really be hurt by something someone said to you—but you are and you keep telling yourself and everyone else that you are not. An intellectual-emotional body is when something happens and you figure out how people want you to feel and then act in that way when all the time you are feeling nothing.

The Emotional Level: Managing The Gift

There are four specific things that seem to help with this impact: *Healthy Perspectives, Cleaning Out, Identifying & Deconstructing* and *Emotional Coffee Breaks*.

Healthy Perspectives

Before you can help someone distinguish and work with the A.D.D. impact or the intellectual-emotional level, you need to check on their own beliefs, insights and feelings about emotions. Now remember, due to the A.D.D. impact, the feelings about emotions are likely to be skewed in the first place, much like Brian's were in the earlier example. After I explain to people what has been happening in their emotional level and make sure that they have a good handle on it, I then begin helping them to understand the emotional level itself. I also help them figure out what they saw role modeled to them about emotions. Have they made them all about their gender? Do they see them as handicaps in general? Do they come from a place where their emotional level is their enemy? We must help them to see and understand what it means to have a healthy emotional level, why they need one and why, at this point in the game, they might even want one. During this process, it is important to understand why the emotional level itself is a gift. In fact, having a healthy emotional body can be one of the all-time greatest gifts in your life.

Cleaning Out

When you begin to work with someone on the issues surrounding the emotional level, it is also a good time to deal with any anger, resentment and pent-up emotions. If that seems like it would be dichotomous to the concept that people just get rid of all their emotions when they explode, it is not. Like the person who is shoving down their emotions, the person with the A.D.D.

impact is often trying (at the very least), to minimize the emotions when they do have a drop. But they have the leftover emotions and wounds there already about a great many other issues that they have chosen to avoid. These are a good example of festering wounds.

When you are experiencing this process, you may find that you are touching upon the unresolved issues surrounding the way you have been treated in a situation over which you had no control. The resentment may not only be about the treatment, but also about the people involved. It is interesting the number people who come to some intellectual understanding that someone—parent, brother, sister, even schoolteacher—was doing the best they could and then they think that realization is the end of it. They then find out that the memories of the traumas, comments and actions still need to be addressed from the emotional standpoint. The hurt still happened. The feeling of being unlovable still happened. The feeling of being broken still happened. The feeling of abandonment still happened. Whatever feelings were created due to these events still happened and no intellectualizations are going to release that reality. It happened and the feelings need to be addressed. So, to get all of this working like the gift it is you must touch and release the struggle. In order to move forward, you must clean out the slime from your emotional level.

Identifying & Deconstructing

The best approach to identifying and deconstructing the intellectual-emotional level is to track it back to any memories you may have of when you created it. I hope that after reading this book, you will feel safe enough and better enough about yourself to allow yourself to access that understanding. The earlier you started constructing this response and the more painful the memories surrounding it, the harder it can be. In the next section, we are going to talk about how to access those emotions and be able to have them in a healthy way. That will help the process of healing.

When writing this book, I deliberated about whether or not to place the *Identifying and Deconstructing* section or the *Emotional Coffee Break* section first. Some people cannot even begin to think about owning or letting go of their intellectual-emotional level. It is something that is like a security blanket. It helps them maintain the illusion of normalcy. Sometimes the person you are most deceiving with the illusion is yourself because you want so much to be 'normal' and fit in. If this level disappears, what will replace it? Whether you start dissecting before or after you start the using the *Emotional Coffee Breaks,* you must understand the importance of dissecting the *intellectual-emotional level.*

To do this, you must stop every time you have an emotion about something and see if you are truly feeling it or if you are simply eliciting the proper response. Pay attention if things happen and you are flat lining. Flat lining is a place where you are having no emotions, no reactions or responses to anything that is happening. What is the difference between truly feeling and eliciting a response? Are there situations or people you feel you have to have emotional responses to, even if you do not feel them? Also, review the section on what healthy emotional bodies look like and what they do not look like. Make sure you know the difference between an internal processing style, shutting down and flat lining. The sooner you dissect it the better. If you need to go back to the earlier section in this chapter and make sure you have identified your processing style. It creates stress and takes a lot of time and energy to juggle two emotional levels. Most people have enough struggles with just trying to deal with one!

Emotional Coffee Breaks

Before I even explain this to you, I want you to understand that I have many clients doing this. It can be done and it does help. I have clients from eleven to over sixty years of age who have had success, but it takes some practice and you have to work at it.

Emotional Coffee Breaks are best done at a regular time. This time should reflect your drop pattern. You go into the place where the energies are being held and bring them out one at a time. Have the emotion, decide what you need to do with the emotion, take any necessary action to resolve the emotion and then let it go. You are draining off the emotions before they get a chance to drop on you. I have created a step by step list of procedures on how to do an emotional coffee break.

The Emotional Coffee Break Procedure

1. Establish a schedule based upon your drop pattern. Determine whether you are someone who holds twelve or fifteen emotions in the emotional holding tank before they drop or just five or six. Obviously, if you drop after five or six, you will have to do emotional coffee breaks more often.

2. When you have the coffee break, begin a mental review of everything that has transpired since your last coffee break. What you are looking for are exchanges, incidents or anything else where an emotion would have been created that is sitting in your holding tank.

3. List any event that you know might have created energy. Review the event, what happened and what was said or done.

4. Intellectually decide what emotion or emotions would have been created.

5. Go in and touch the emotion. Do not intellectualize it. Touch it. Let your knowledge of how it feels lead you to the feeling.

6. If more than one feeling comes out around the issue, list all of them. Acknowledge each one of them separately. Allow yourself to say the feeling aloud, three times, with the energy that is attached to it: i.e. *"I feel hurt"* or *"I feel angry."* Do not deadpan it. Allow the feeling to flow out.

7. After you have honored and accepted all the individual feelings associated with that event, sort them into the following categories:

- you and anyone else involved in the event
- you and another person unrelated to the actual event
- you and yourself
- you and an old, unresolved issue

8.   Now, begin to process, maybe even journal on what emotions are related to feelings you have towards yourself. If the emotion is attached to an earlier experience or string of experiences, that means they have never been resolved within you. If you cannot journal and work on the other two, schedule time when you can.

9.   If you feel that the issue is something that you can identify but do not know what or how to resolve it, then find someone else to help you process it.

10.   Now decide on any action that you need to take with any person who was involved with the issue.

11.   Next, decide on any action that you need to take with another person who is unrelated to the event but still related to the feeling.

12.   Move on to the next event. Repeat until done.

If this list seems to overwhelm you but you understand the concept then I will share with you how one of my clients put this list into shorthand with which she could work. She said that when you sit down to review your time between breaks you should do this:

1)   Identify (What had happened that you have energy on?) Steps 1—6

2)   Process (Why do you have energy on it?) Steps 7—9

3)   Act (What are you going to do about it?) Steps 10—12

If you need more instruction than that, then try the list.

This may sound like a long, drawn-out and cumbersome process and it will probably feel like that the first couple of times. The more you do it, however, the quicker and more clearly you learn to determine what is what and what you need to do about it. The more you do these breaks, the fewer other issues will be involved because you will have cleared them out. Then you will stop having drops because the holding tank will be continually siphoned, not dumped.

Time to look at an example.

Mary Jane, mid-forties, has been working at the same company for years and is in a mid-level management position. She has a *hold drop pattern* of 12-6-2. Halfway through her morning, she decides it is time for her to do her emotional coffee break. We will go through one thing that is in her holding tank. First she sits down at her keyboard, (where she prefers doing her coffee breaks) and thinks back to when she did her last coffee break. One of the things she identifies as something that irritates her is an exchange she had with her boss this morning. Recently, she had cut back on her coffee. Before cutting back, she had always been the first in the office, so she always had the coffee made and ready for everyone when they arrived. Now she only has one cup and picks it up on her way in but had continued to still make the coffee when she came in. However, she did not think about doing that this morning. When one of her bosses came in, he told her that she was slipping up on the job and her good coffee was what kept getting her promoted. He then laughed. She knew he was not serious. She knew that light-hearted banter was part of this boss's personality, but as soon as he left she went and made the coffee. In reviewing her morning, this stuck out as something that bothered her. Therefore, she listed it as something that she needed to look at (Step 1—3).

After Mary Jane listed other things, she went on to the next step: deciding what emotions were created. Well, when she thought about the incident she realized the following emotions elicited from that event were: anger, shame, doubt and fear (Step 4). So then Mary Jane sat and allowed herself to feel each of those emotions. She quietly said each of the emotions three times.

"I feel angry, I feel angry, I feel angry." Each time she allowed herself to feel the energy of anger. She moved on to the next one.

"I feel shame, I feel shame, I feel shame." She then sat with that for a moment and moved on to the next emotion.

"I feel doubt, I feel doubt, I feel doubt." Finally, she was ready for the last emotion she felt over this situation.

"I feel fear, I feel fear, I feel fear," but this time she did not feel as though she had really touched the emotions so she did it three more times. "I feel fear, I feel fear, I feel fear." She then felt better (Step 5—6).

Now that she had honored all the feelings she needed to feel, it was time to figure out where those feelings had come from. She went through the different categories of feelings and this is what she realized: She was angry with her boss Dick who often makes such comments to her, indicating that, although she is the highest woman in the company, he wants her to remember her place.

She also figured out that some of the anger had to do with an exchange she had before work with her husband, John. John had taken his anger and guilt out on her because she had not done something that he said he would do and did not get around to doing. In both cases, she was being held accountable for things she had never agreed to do.

She was also angry with herself because she had, in both cases, ended up doing something to placate the situation.

In the case of the shame, doubt and fear, they had nothing to do with either actual situation. The doubt had to do with her relationship with herself. Some part of herself felt unworthy in both her marriage and her job, although she knew better intellectually. This was something she was going to have to look at, think about and journal on later.

As for the shame and fear, she related both of these to her childhood and a parent who always criticized her whenever anything went wrong telling her "if she didn't shape up she would be shipped out." This was something else that she would need to look at in more depth later. (Step 7—8)

And in reviewing the last three emotions, she felt that those were things that she was probably going to need to work through in our next counseling session (Step 9).

Now she was going to have to decide what was the best way to approach Dick and let him know how she felt and why. She could now do this from a centered place instead of a reactionary one (Step 10).

Then she was going to have to decide how she was going to approach John about not taking his self-frustration out on her as if it were her fault (Step 11).

Now she was ready to look at the next thing on her list (Step 12). She had already done quite a bit of work on it, since the item was the discussion she had with her husband that morning.

That is what an emotional coffee break could look like.

The Emotional Level:
Why the A.D.D. Impact is a Gift

As I mentioned earlier, this was the level that I had the hardest time picturing as a gift. I had to put this concept together with everything else that I knew about the emotional level for the gift status to make sense. One of the reasons that we have always been prejudiced against the emotional level is because we felt as though we could not control it; that the emotions were so powerful that they affected us and made us feel powerless. Instead of learning to manage them and, deal with them, we became experts at denying them, suppressing them. Instead of feeling an emotion you feel powerless to control or do anything about, you become separated from that which is creating the emotions. This way you can sort them. And you can deal with them in a safe environment. The process of being able to deal with your emotions this way keeps your emotional body cleaner and clearer.

The gift of having an emotional level impacted by A.D.D. is that instead of having emotions randomly, inconveniently and at a time or place where you cannot easily deal with them, you get to have them in a safe, convenient time and place of your choice.

You can do emotional coffee breaks as often as necessary, allowing yourself to both have your emotions and do so when it is most convenient. You can also, in a centered way, decide on any actions that you need to take and take them so that emotions are not building up. You can deal with your emotions fully, but on your schedule instead of by chance. You drastically decrease the possibility of someone egging you on to do something foolish or engaging you in a fight. Emotions can wreak havoc in what we are trying to accomplish at any given moment. Even when we are taking the energy to shove them back down, they distract us, take us off focus and drain us. How often have you been in the middle of your day when an incident happens that brings up a great deal of emotions and then suddenly your day is shot? At the very least, you have to stop and regroup. With an emotional coffee break, you get to sort. You get to understand what you were feeling and why.

When used properly, the emotional level of someone with A.D.D. is much more efficient and user-friendly than the old variety. You can have your emotions in a timely manner and in a fashion that is not destructive or self-destructive. You get to utilize your emotional level to its fullest potential.

Summary For The Emotional Level

After centuries of letting emotions bring us the incredible highs, endless passions and beautiful visions, as well as the wars, fears and irrational choices that have sometimes led to death and destruction, we finally get to do it differently. We have developed a way to combine the intellectual and emotional levels, to get the good part of emotions and have a much better way of dealing with the disruptive and destructive part. Of course, centuries of habits die-hard and there will still be those who think that they can keep emotions an intellectual exercise. They will still pay the price.

Emotional drop patterns make dealing with emotions look more attractive and efficient. Of course, this method requires the ability to be honest with yourself about your own feelings and your own baggage. Remember that if we develop a continuous cleaning system for our emotions, we may (in a couple of genera-tions) severely limit the amount of garbage that we are creating and passing on.

Chapter 4
Intellectual Level

The intellectual level is how we think and what we think.
It contains both our potential and our actual (what we have done
with it so far). In it, we can see what the possibilities are as well as
what is actually happening. We learn to discern and to judge
through it. We learn new things and become stuck in old ones. It
is the place from which we perform the majority of our verbal
communications. We associate symbols with labels and we learn
the labels assigned to those symbols—not always the same thing.
Sometimes we even allow ourselves to come up with our own
labels for those symbols. It is not uncommon for twins to develop their own language when young and two people who are
close will have inside jokes. They even may develop shorthand
that, to the outside world, is a language of its own.

The intellectual level is often where we decide or are
taught what to feel about any number of things. What we think is
the easiest thing to explain and understand: our beliefs and our
opinions. What we think is dictated by what we have been exposed to, what we have been taught, what we are drawn to explore, to learn and to experience. Earlier I used the word 'simply.'
Unfortunately, it may start as simple concepts, but we complicate
things quickly. The discussion of how we think indicates both the

next section, remember the importance of knowing who you are and be able to differentiate between what is being affected by the A.D.D. and what is just an extension of who you are. If you are reading this book to support someone who has A.D.D., help that person to determine his or her *styles*. As you read, you will note that there are obvious styles of learning and thinking that have a tendency to be supported both in the school system and by expectations associated with gender. When you work with your A.D.D. or someone else's A.D.D., make sure you do not try to become or have them become something that they are not.

The Intellectual Level:
What has it been designed to do

Our intellectual level was designed to reason, to vision and to analyze. It was created to be both a recorder and a communicator of our human experience. It is both the master and servant to our physical level, our emotional level and our spiritual level.

First, how do we think? I am going to break it down into categories that I will call *styles*. There are learning , processing and thinking styles. When we get to the A.D.D. impact, our understanding of these styles will help us differentiate between the challenges brought about by A.D.D. and environmental issues that are being blamed on the A.D.D.

Learning Styles

There have been many books written on styles of learning, covering a multitude of combinations and tangential learning styles. For our purposes, we will look at three basic learning styles: *auditory, visual* and *kinesthetic*. Of course, there are combinations of the three.

Auditory Learning

Auditory learning is the kind of learning style where hearing is the easiest and most efficient way for someone to understand or grasp a concept. When the person with this learning style becomes quiet, pays attention and listens, they will learn or understand what is being taught. You might identify this type by observing them when they are trying to understand something difficult. It is not unusual for them to close their eyes, even tilt their head as if they are trying to tune their ear in to hear you and tune out everything else around them. If you give the auditory learner directions, they will listen intently, repeat them back to you and then go. If you change anything in the directions after the auditory learner repeats them to you, they will assimilate the changes and most likely repeat the whole thing over again with the corrected information. Hearing themselves say it commits the information to memory.

Visual Learning

Visual learning involves seeing something it in order to best comprehend it. They see it on the blackboard or read it in a book or even write it down. These learners may be copious note-takers, not only for what is written on the board but also for whatever the teacher says. They may never actually read the notes because the act of committing it to paper is enough. If you give this person directions they will write them down and they may even draw a map. When they drive, they may never look at the directions because seeing them written down was enough.

Kinesthetic Learning

Kinesthetic learners learn by doing and interacting. If you can involve them in the process, that is how they understand it. Kinesthetic learning is linked to kinetics, the energy of movement. If there is movement involved, the kinesthetic learner does better, even if the movement is yours. If you show them how to do something by doing it, it is more helpful than telling them, giving them something to read about it or writing it on the board. If you give this person directions, they are likely to be tracing the movements in midair or on a table. Their hands may be making left and right motions or any other gestures that help commit the energy to memory.

In my years in corporate America, I often held training or training manager positions. I learned that the best way to do standard training was this:

- Have them read about what you are getting. ready to training them on.
- Then tell them what you are going to tell them.
- Tell them.
- Show them.
- Then tell them what you told them.

You follow this by:

- Having them tell you what you told them.
- Then show you what you showed them.
- The ultimate step in the process is to observe. them teaching someone else.

Depending on what you are teaching, the process is sometimes easy but other times it is a far more creative one. This is an extremely efficient teaching method as it incorporates all three learning styles. Most people have a primary and secondary learning style. Although they both work one will always be more effective. I will not say that success is ensured with this training style, but the success rate is high. The big factor 'x' in these scenarios has nothing to do with ability. It is usually about desire. Someone who wants to learn something, conscious or unconsciously, will lead you to the learning style they need—if you let them. They may ask questions, or ask for something to read or ask you to show and work with them. If the chore of learning becomes too difficult or too cumbersome, they will lose interest.

Processing Styles

There are two basic styles of processing: *introvert* and

extrovert. These styles have nothing to do with personality or whether the person is outgoing or shy. Unfortunately, this seems to be an automatic assumption. Because I have a very outgoing personality, people often assume that I am an extrovert in my processing style. Because my partner keeps more to himself, they assume that he has an introverted processing style. It is just the reverse! In fact, we were at a conference a few years ago and one of the other people there was studying iridology, the science of receiving information about a person through the study of their eyes. She asked if she could look into our eyes and tell us what she saw. On other occasions and through the four days of the conference, she had spent a fair amount of social time with us. She first looked into my eyes and then without saying anything called my partner over, looked into his eyes and then looked at both of us again. With that, she then told us, with a fair amount of surprise in her voice, that I was the introvert and my partner was the extrovert. We confirmed her information, since we had already figured that out. So, what do I mean when I talk about introverts and extroverts when it comes to processing styles?

Extrovert

Someone with an *extrovert* processing style likes to think through things by getting them outside of themselves. In other words, they need to talk it through with someone else to figure out what they are thinking and feeling about something. The funny thing is that it is not unusual for the other person not to say anything at all! It is simply the act of processing or working through something aloud that helps the extrovert. Sometimes they want input and other times they just need to get it out. When they have reached some kind of conclusion which is acceptable and manageable in their own mind, they can then open up and get input. If you try to give them input too quickly, it will distract them from their own processes and they will likely either snap at you or shut down. The extrovert is the person who becomes stuck in their head and needs to literally 'get out of their head' so they can sort through something. By giving them more or new information, they end up back in their head with the information and are in danger of being stuck again. This is especially true of people who have a tendency to be caught in thought loops. A thought loop is an idea or set of ideas to which you keep returning—you seem unable to break the loop. One of the harder parts of the extrovert processing style is that it takes someone a very long time (if it ever does happen) to figure out and be able to ask the person that they are processing with to give them what they need. This is because they do not understand what it is that they need. That makes it tough. So oftentimes, the person dealing with an extroverted processing style will try to 'fix' the problems instead of just hearing them out. This continues until the extrovert gets to a point where they are specifically asking for feedback. In addition, in this processing style they can contradict themselves many times before they finally come to the point of resolution. This creates even more confusion for the listener.

Introvert

An *introvert* processes things internally. When something occurs about which they are unresolved, they go within them-selves. There are two kinds of internal processing; one is con-scious and the other is unconscious. Conscious internal process-ing involves the person working through it within his or her own head, weighing pros and cons and then coming to some kind of decision or conclusion. The person with the unconscious style of internal processing may or may not weigh some pros and cons, but they do not consciously come to a conclusion or a decision. It is as if they forget about it or put it out of their mind and then suddenly they 'know' how they feel about something, what they have decided or what conclusion they have reached.

This does not mean the person with an introvert-process-ing pattern does not get additional information or consult other people, but the real work happens within their mind. Sometimes they might be asking questions or steering conversations in certain directions with no concept as to why. They are just gathering information.

Looking at these styles, you can see how an outgoing person who is very friendly might be an introverted processor. Though someone might be quiet or soft spoken, they might actually process in an extroverted way.

Thinking Styles

For our purposes, we will talk about two styles of thinking: *analytical* and *abstract*. These are often associated with masculine and feminine energy. This is not wholly incorrect, but it does not have anything to do with being male or female.

Analytical

Analytical thinking is sequential in nature. It is also associated with logical thinking. It is left brain thinking and deals well with things that fall into some kind of orderly or discernable pattern. It is a thinking style that is very action orientated. It tries to make everything orderly, practical and logical. The focus tends to be much more solution orientated, with the goals tending towards those things that are simple, quick and efficient. Analytical thinking is definitely a style that is much more comfortable with a 'black and white' reality. It will often reject that which has not or can not be proven.

Abstract

Abstract thinking is a style geared towards probabilities and possibilities as much as facts. The abstract thinker pairs things together, which may have no logical connections. They are much more willing to follow hunches and see where these hunches will take them rather than being content with what the facts indicate. Creative and inventive, their road to a solution may be hard, if not impossible, to follow. This does not make it any less likely to be correct, just harder to explain. They are less interested in the 'what' of a situation and more interested in the 'why.' It is not the surface 'why' they are interested in but the deeper 'why.'

As you look over some of the protocols that I have created or you try to create protocols for your self keep these *styles* in mind. Make sure that you are not trying to create a reality of something that you are not or try to modify something that is just part of who you are and needs to not be changed but accepted and worked with.

The Intellectual Level:
The box we have created for it

Now, let us look at what myths and dysfunctional realities we have created around the many communication styles. We will first look at what we have created around the intellectual level in general and then we will discuss the specific styles.

In general, we have genderized intelligence, making certain kinds of intelligence or intellectual pursuits more acceptable for males and others for females. We have also prized certain kinds of intellect, learning, processing, and thinking styles over others. We have role modeled and rewarded inappropriate styles and behaviors. We have also created educational, social and workplace structures that are prejudiced and punishing to those who do not have the 'prized kinds,' oftentimes associating style with ability, an incorrect association. We put a high value on what we recognize in our current system as intelligent and often stigmatize those with alternative styles; which affects their self-worth and self-esteem.

We have created educational systems geared toward audio/visual learners. If your primary two learning styles are not audio and visual, you work with an unfair disadvantage. Depending on the grade, subject and the teacher's teaching style, one kind of learning style will be far more beneficial than the other one will. If you are primarily a kinesthetic learner, you are out of luck until maybe high school. You will have to work harder, get tutors or find creative ways of teaching yourself. You probably will not do as well as a student, on the same level, who is an audio/visual learner. You are then graded, labeled and placed in certain groups, all of which communicate to you that you are not as bright as your peers are. Of course, kinesthetic learners learn better through interacting or in motion. This can add to their separation and labeling process. All of this increases the potential for damaging and negative self-imaging. It can also affect the directions in which these students are guided and what they are led to believe they are or are not capable of accomplishing or pursuing. We link learning style and the ability to regurgitate information as the primary measurements of intelligence it is not.

We have, in this culture, tended to assign both gender and an indication of strength to our concept of our processing style. It is somehow stronger and more masculine to sort it out yourself, to come to your own conclusion. We have considered the need to 'talk' about everything or talk everything out as feminine and a sign of a weak mind or a weak character that needs someone stronger to guide them. In reviewing both styles, each has its own way of acquiring information. Talking about a situation is no indication that you need any guidance or that you need someone else to make your decision. Because someone does not struggle outwardly with something does not mean they do not struggle. Oftentimes, it can be an internal struggle—a situation that can be much more painful. The mythology we have created around this is a bunch of happy horse manure.

I have avoided expressing any opinion about whether the analytical or abstract processing style is the best or most preferable, but there is a clear, hands-down choice. First, however, let us look at what we have done with our thinking styles. We clearly associate each of the two styles with one gender or the other. The male is more the practical, analytical and logical in nature. The female is more abstract, creative, free flowing and emotional. Unless they have reached some level of success, popularity, prestige or power, we tend to belittle, harass and look down on people with styles we have decided are more appropriate for the other gender.

Now, for the hands down winner of the 'which is the best style of thinking' contest: *both*. As needed. We all have the capacity to be both left and right brained and there are experiences in our lives that would be best handled by being able to move from one to the other. Everybody has masculine energy.

Everybody has feminine energy. The balance of that energy will continually change throughout your lifetime. The best balance of the masculine/feminine energy is one where is changes from moment to moment as the situation demands it. Unfortunately, however, often what energy someone is in has little to do with what would be best or most appropriate but much more to do with conditioning. Keeping this in mind, it is time to examine the A.D.D. impact on the intellectual level.

The Intellectual Level:
The A.D.D. Impact.

The intellectual level is impacted three ways by the A.D.D. factor: first in the *amount* of information that it can receive, second in the *way* the information is received and third in the way the intellectual level *needs to process* the information it receives.

Amount of Information

It has traditionally been estimated that the average person uses about 10% of their brain's capacity. The A.D.D. impact has increased the ability of the brain from that 10% usage to a 15% to 20% usage. We have always known that the ability of the brain is severely underutilized, but now we have reached an evolutionary point where we as a culture, instead of just the occasional individual, need to literally expand the brain. We need to have more access to it in order to keep expanding in all other areas of our lives. For you computer people out there, we need to access more of the hard drive and need more RAM in order to run all the programs necessary to live our daily lives and keep growing. In the computer world, there is a concept of partitioning off your hard drive. If you have a very large hard drive, you partition it into smaller, more easily accessible drives. You can then keep more things stored with more organization and structure. You can divide information by considering how often and how much you need certain things accessible. Well, the brain is the human equivalent of a **very** large hard drive. Some of that hard drive is used up in the operating system, but much of it is partitioned off for subconscious use, storage and potential future use. We have now reached the time to make more of the hard drive available on a wider scale. That's evolution for you!

How information is received

I am going to continue with the computer analogy for a bit longer. Take a minute and think about what it is like when you are working on your computer. You open the main operating system—Windows, for example. Then you have to open the program you would like to use, let us say Word. Now you have to open the document you want to work on in Word; however, this is a document into which you want to put graphics. Well, now you open a graphics program. The document you are working on is one into which you are eventually going to scan something, so you need to have the scanner program open. If you have a really good computer, you do not have to worry that you are going to reach a point where everything is going to freeze because you simply do not have enough RAM to deal with all the things you must open. If you do heavy graphics work or some other work which is memory intensive, a good computer knows how to organize and run what you need in a way that will maximize the efficiency, keep it running quickly and not lead to shut downs.

The A.D.D. impact creates the 'opening of more pro-grams.' These people have more information coming into their brain and it is coming in differently. Therefore, the management of this information needs to be different. In the work I have done so far, the reception of information falls into four catego-ries. I call them *Spaghetti, Pulse, Burst* and *Mongrel.*

Spaghetti

Spaghetti is when all the information hangs down at once. When I see it energetically, it is like massive amounts of spaghetti hanging down, with each strand representing a thought string. For the computer person it would be like having every program on your computer open at once. Scary, huh? Well, for that person the mind is a place of seduction. It is a wonderland of thoughts to be followed, possibilities to be explored, adventures to take. This person loves to learn and gets very easily distracted within themselves when whatever is going on around them loses their interest. This is the original daydreamer, magnified a hundred times. If you can keep their attention, they will stay with you because, for the most part, they have a natural love of learning. If they did not, they would not be so seduced by their own mind. These children and adults are like wine connoisseurs who have a cellar full of expensive, priceless vintage wines at their disposal. They want to try and savor them while the world at large attempts to keep their attention with an occasional good wine but usually just a great deal of 'jug' wine. It just does not compare. And the more this mind matures the more it resents having to spend its time on 'jug' wine when it has already developed a taste for the 'good stuff.'

Pulse

The *Pulse* pattern occurs when the information comes in waves. Thoughts or ideas come in groups or clusters at regular intervals. Instead of managing several different ideas at any given moment as most of us do, they may get four or five times as many things coming into their reality in waves. It would be like opening four or five documents at a time instead of one. If one thing is not holding their attention, many other things have come into their reality to which they can then turn their attention. Unlike *Spaghetti,* where there are many options all the time, things 'pop up' in the pulse pattern. It is easy to be distracted by these 'new' thoughts especially if what you are focusing on is no longer interesting. This is like when you sit in a restaurant and hear the same story for the fifteenth time. You suddenly realize that within earshot are a half dozen other conversations. The conversations may not even be interesting or comprehensible to you, the out-sider, but at least they are new; so you scan around and see if any of them hold your attention. This goes on both internally and externally in the A.D.D. impacted person. For the child who understands something the first time the teacher explains it, the next five times the teacher repeats it so the other children can get it, loses their attention. With the *Spaghetti* pattern, they will just daydream. With the pulse, they are likely to first scan around them to see if there is anything more interesting or if they have just had an input of new information they can focus on. Next, they are likely to want to share those 'new' thoughts because they are far more interesting than hearing for the fifth time how to do something. Where both of these children get lost is that sometimes they teacher moves on and they are so caught up in their own 'world' that they do not acknowledge the change. Then they lose some piece of information that they need to continue the process. We will go more into that later in the book.

<u>*Burst*</u>

Burst is an explosion of thoughts, ideas and/or questions that overwhelms the person with this pattern. This is when the mind suddenly opens and is flooded with information. This person will sometimes be so overwhelmed that they may actually shut down for a moment or they will suddenly try talking and it seems like they cannot make comprehensible sentences. For this person, it may take periods of time to be able to sort through everything that was released in their mind. When one of these bursts happens, they become *mentally hyperactive.* Trying to put in any additional information will only continue to overload them.

It often seems as if some comprehension or realization will trigger a burst. When the floodgates open, everything that comes out will somehow be correlated to the insight or realizations. It may not always be easy to see the correlation, but it is there. This person may struggle and struggle to understand how some concept or idea works. Suddenly the light turns on and they 'get it.' Upon getting the insight, the burst will occur and many other thoughts, ideas or concepts pour forth, flooding the mind. The leaps can be amazingly abstract and insights profound. We have always had members of the human race who seem to have this ability to suddenly go from struggle and failure to a brilliant insight and success. Many times this is referred to as 'something clicks.' For the person with this kind of A.D.D. impacted intellectual level it is feast or famine. Not getting it, not getting it, not getting it and then getting it big time—with a whole lot more.

Continuing our computer analogy here, this pattern is when you are putting together something very complicated on your computer, something which may need to draw upon information from more than one source in order to work. In putting it together, you may be downloading something from the Internet, accessing the CD-ROM drive and using more than one program. You then sit there waiting and waiting and waiting. You keep looking at the timer, making sure it is still working, knowing how delicate and fussy this whole process can be and how one key stroke at the wrong time can throw the whole thing off. Then your final product suddenly appears and is even more than you expected.

Mongrel

The *Mongrel* pattern mixes up two or more of the other three patterns. When a mongrel pattern is present, the severity of the other three is lessened. In this case, the person may have many threads always hanging and available while the incoming information comes in a pulse pattern and then occasionally they will have a burst. This is the child or adult who sits there, easily given to daydreaming, and intellectually restless. They may ask many questions and will occasionally become mentally hyperactive. They may seem as if they will burst if they cannot talk; and with the amount of information flowing through them at that moment, they just might. Trying to stop or hold all the rushing mental energy could lead to severe headaches, possible migraines or even nausea.

Processing the information

Because of the amount and way that the information is received, getting it out of the head in order to understand it is usually the best way to process it. These people are more likely to need to be external processors of one kind or another. If they do not actually need to just spill it all out when they are overloaded, then they are likely to need to write it down in some fashion. It is almost like the need to dump it in order to use it. Once it has been dumped than it can be sorted, put in some kind of order and reason can be made out of the chaos. This most clearly applies to the *Burst* pattern. For the *Pulse*, depending on the intensity of the pulse, more of the organizing of things might be able to be done in the head or by writing. With the *Spaghetti*, writing might be used more of the time for the sorting and organizing of thoughts.

The Intellectual Level: Managing The Gift

It is here that the gift is clearest: the increased ability to access, use and process more information than ever before in the current known history of the world. The ability of the A.D.D. impacted person to take us into new realms of thoughts, realities and understandings is incredible. The difficulty that lies before that person is two-fold: first, getting them to successfully explore and utilize those abilities and second, to overcome the archaic ways in which a majority of school systems and social systems work- ways which often victimize them.

There are several techniques to help deal with the increased flow of incoming information. These are some of the things that my clients have found helpful:

> *Checklists*
> *'Things To Do' lists*
> *Putting it in writing*
> *Notebooks*
> *Learning while in motion*

Timed learning
Auditory learning
Once through, hurry please
Structure, structure, structure

Before this section is through, I will have either said, inferred or reiterated this simple baseline understanding of the person who is impacted by A.D.D. in their intellectual level: they have so much going on in their head that it needs to be organized. It takes so much energy for them to hyperfocus on what they are doing that they need *very* regular breaks from any kind of mental activity that is not *extremely* intellectually stimulating. Let us see how the list I just gave you plays into either or both of those concepts.

Checklists

Remember how we have talked about the seductive nature of the brain and how the A.D.D. impacted person can get 'lost' within his or her own head? So, you need checklists; sometimes, very specific checklist about what needs to be done and even sometimes how it needs to be done. For the rest of us, learning something as simple as how to clean the bathroom is a piece of cake. We may not be particularly drawn to want to clean the bathroom, but we listen, learn and then memorize. Our active brain is not so active that this is that much of a chore. For the A.D.D. impacted person, however, learning can often be very easy, but the memorization part throws them because things that have not truly interested them get very easily lost in the minutiae of their brain. This *is not* a case of willing forgetfulness. It simply does not register. Threatening them does nothing within the thought process of the brain to make an uninteresting piece of information interesting. The piece literally goes in and gets lost in the great chaotic whirl of thoughts, ideas and other pieces of information. If it is something learned, thought through and then attached to a process, it is much more easily found and accessed. So the A.D.D. impacted person must sit down, hyperfocus and create a checklist of things that they need to make sure are done on a daily basis. For the parent, spouse or other individual involved with the A.D.D. impacted person, you can help them create this checklist, making it as complete and detailed as it needs to be. Here is an actual story of a family with whom I worked to help a twelve-year-old child impacted with A.D.D.:

I spent ten days with this family to help them and their child with the A.D.D. impact. One of the things which aggravated the mother was that she worked and only asked the child to do one chore a day when he got home from school: clean the bathroom. On a daily basis, she would come home from work and the child would be playing a game or watching television and the bathroom would not be cleaned. No matter how much she cajoled, threatened, yelled or punished the child, the bathroom was not being cleaned or was being cleaned very poorly.

When speaking to the young man, once I was through his protective indifference, he broke down crying, admitting that there were times when he sat in the middle of the bathroom floor, in tears, wanting to remember what to do and how to do it and just could not remember. The instructions had never fully registered in his brain and he was so afraid of his parents finding out how 'stupid' he was that he would just pretend that he had forgotten. After speaking with the mother and father we created a checklist that included reminders of not only what to do but how to do it. It has not been a problem since.

Notebooks

There is a two-fold purpose to notebooks. One is for the adult who should always carry a notebook in an attaché case, pocketbook, backpack, fanny pack or whatever you take everywhere you go. In it you can fold up, attach or paper clip your daily to do checklist. You will also have a place to write down any thoughts, ideas, or 'I forgot to do's' right into a section of the notebook for that purpose. Then, every night you go through that section and you put everything where it belongs (the 'To Do List,' the checklist, etc.) and take it out of your notebook.

The second purpose of the notebook is for the student to keep open when they are in class or the businessperson to keep open when they are in meetings. As errant thoughts or ideas begin to take their focus, they can just jot down one or two words or a phrase to help them remember. They can then get back to these notes at a later time and not get as distracted from what is going on, as well as not losing what might be an important thread of an idea.

Things To Do Lists

So now that you have started to create specific checklists for specific tasks. In addition, you have a notebook to place things as they come up during the day to take your attention away. Now the next two things to create are two 'Things To Do' lists: a master and daily.

The master list will include anything done on a regular basis, but not daily. It should always be looked at from a priority basis, to see what needs to be transferred to the daily list and sometimes on to the checklist. The master to do list is also the list for things you suddenly think of, or come up, that do not need to be done immediately or even in the same day, but do need to be done. You put things from your notebook on this list at the end of day. For a child or an adult who has a difficulty ascertaining what is and is not a priority, a parent, spouse, teacher or friend may want to get involved in the process or be available as a sounding board. Depending on the age, period of life and re-sponsibility level of the individual, some things may just transfer directly over to the daily checklist or may be broken up.

So you now have a daily to do list, which is created every morning or the night before, of what you need to do as well as what you can get done (depending on how busy your day is). So, for a student, your daily to do list would be things you can do before and after school or following after-school activities. It includes anything that you can do during the school day between classes. Things that might be on it would be daily chores, homework, calling a friend to see about plans to get together this weekend, some part of a project that you are working on and maybe to get air in the tires of your bike. After the school day, the things to do list needs to be reviewed, in order to take in account how much time new homework will take. If it is a heavy homework day, there may be something that slides back onto the master to do list, as something to be done on another day. If it was an extremely light homework day, you might look to get something else off your master things to do list or you may use the extra time as down time. There should always be some down time factored in.

For the adult, it may be a longer master to do things list and even a longer daily things to do list. In some ways, however, it is easier because you do not need to change it after school each day. Most days you only need to do it once.

I will give examples of this from actual clients.

Example #1

One college student with whom I was working had a problem with becoming overwhelmed by the amount of homework she had to do. I already had her on a checklist that was helping her immensely in her daily life. In the checklist she just had a line item that said, 'Do homework.' I then had her do a master 'to do list' that only involved her homework, projects and papers. It also included the due dates of reading assignments and a schedule of studying for tests.

At the close of every school day, she would include any new assignments that had been added. I also had her break up any larger assignments into small, manageable groups to not overwhelm her. She would enter her homework that needed to be the next day into her daily to do list. Everything else was entered into her master to do list. Looking over her

daily to do list, if it were a light homework assignment list,
she would then add things from her master list until it was
a moderate homework day. By doing this, she rarely ended
up with the heavy homework days that were overwhelming
her.

Example #2

This is an example from a family with whom I
worked who had two children in junior high school, one of
the children, Josh, was impacted with A.D.D. and one child
was not. In this case, one of the big issues was the comple-
tion of chores. So first, we created a list explaining what
the chores were and how they need to be done. Next we
created a master list of chores, and how they were to bet
dispersed throughout the family. The list reflected time of
year and outside commitments. Both Josh and his brother
participated in the creation of the lists. Then all the chores
were divided and listed on the appropriate daily to do list,
for both Josh and his brother.

So Josh's daily checklist for Monday might have
been:

1.　*Do your homework*
2.　*Pick up your room*
3.　*Do the dishes*
4.　*Additional chores:*

Daily checklist for Tuesday:

1.　*Do your homework*
2.　*Do the dishes.*
3.　*Vacuum the living room.*
4.　*Additional chores:*

During the school year, both Josh and his brother
were involved in extra-curricular activities, so the parent
worked with the children dividing the chores in a different

order during the week to compensate for the activities. It may sound cumbersome at first, but it was far clearer and less aggravating for everyone involved once it was created and maintained. Things got done-no more threats or frustrations. The lists were always monitored for school flow, work flow and activity flow.

For example, for several Thursdays in a row Josh had an extracurricular activity that ran into the evening. This did not leave enough time to do chores and homework. So for that period, his Thursday chores were distributed over Monday, Tuesday, Wednesday and Friday. This child also had a separate checklist for schoolwork from which he would draw the homework items for his daily checklist. This same set-up can work for the adult who has difficulty remembering to get everything done.

Putting it in writing

Because there is so much activity going on within the mind and there is a constant influx of incoming information or outflow of ideas playing leapfrog, you must put things in writing. Think about the absent-minded professor type, the one who could look you right in the eye when you are telling them something, repeat what it was you said and still forget it. Well, they are the parents and grandparents of the A.D.D. impacted person—the person who has so much on their mind that when something new goes *in* it gets lost immediately. Whenever you need something done, add it to their 'Things To Do' list or their checklist, write it in their notebook or put it on a piece of paper in their hands (the last choice). Do not just tell them in passing and expect it to happen. The reason I say that putting a piece of paper in their hands or even a sticky note on the dashboard is the last choice is that they will forget to look at it. So, put it on something that they have gotten into the habit of checking, such as their computer screen, the refrigerator or the television. Both the A.D.D. individual and the people around them must learn to put things in writing.

Learning while in motion

One of the ways in which learning something may be facilitated is through learning in motion. If you are having a hard time getting a concept through to an A.D.D. impacted person, explain it while walking, jogging, on the treadmill or even riding in the car. This has as much to do with the rhythm of the physical energy as the rhythm of the intellectual energy and it works. Let them pace or allow them to walk through solutions. As the teacher or trainer, even being more animated and moving around using gestures, modulating the voice or creating the sensation of motion will sometimes help.

Timed learning

Because learning can be such a hyperfocused activity that literally exhausts the A.D.D. impacted person, creating the reality of frequent breaks helps. They need breaks where they get to release the excess energy they have built up and give their hyperfocus a rest. This is extremely powerful during the process of doing homework. Homework seems to be a consistent issue for the A.D.D. impacted person, unless the homework totally fascinates and challenges them. For all of the children and adults I have worked with who have homework or work at home issues, I have set up the following: do 'x' amount of work and then 'x' amount of break. Use an egg timer if necessary. If you are working and the egg timer goes off, just finish whatever you are doing to its logical conclusion.

I often find that the break may involve computer games or physical activity or television. Each has a benefit. Many computer games will create the sensation of movement, as well as challenge the mind in a different way. The physical activity burns off the excess, built-up energy and allows the mind to wander. The television creates the illusion of activity for the brain, when in actuality the 'brain candy' that is often on television allows the mind to rest.

Auditory Learning

Auditory learning can often be helpful because it allows the person to shut out the visual stimuli and relax into the spoken messages or information. Auditory learning can also be used as a way to learn while moving. In many cases, I have had the person tape classes, in which they are having difficulty, get a book tape or tape their class notes onto a tape. They then take the tape and pop it into a Walkman while they are doing some kind of exercise or getting ready to sleep, or even as noise when they are playing computer games.

Once through, hurry please

When they are in hyperfocus mode, this individual has a high capacity for learning. Presenting concepts in one steady stream at a rapid pace is sometimes the best way to present the information. Once you have presented the information to the individual, question them, see if they got it and if they did, then leave them alone and let them do something else. If they did not get it, then find out where they are stuck, address that issue and that issue only, give them a minute and then check again. If they are stuck on something in the middle and you feel like you need to start at the beginning repeatedly, you will lose them. And let them ask the questions they need to ask. So, when explaining something to this person, if they are in a group, go over things quickly, then ask them to repeat the concept to you to see if they have it and if they do, excuse them from the group.

Structure, structure, structure

Structure for this person is like a safety net. Their internal intellectual world is a wild, wonderful adventure; but it is not always a safe place because they can easily get lost within it. In doing so, they can lose track of or not get things that they need to keep living in the mundane world. Creating habits and patterns that will become the structure to make sure they get what they need is what is most helpful. However, you cannot move immediately or too quickly to a place of structure or the A.D.D. impacted person will either sabotage the structure or refuse to use it. This will depend on how scared they have already become because of their treatment from the outside world. This includes issues of self-worth, anger management and unresolved resentments, as well as feelings of powerlessness and inadequacy. At all costs, do not work with these people from a place of condescension. It is an invitation to them to revolt. Imagine how it would feel to have someone 'talk down' to you when you had not received all the information on how to do something or part of the information was in a foreign language that you did not understand. What if you knew whatever they were trying to explain to you was something that, in your own language, you might know better than they did?

The best way to deal with the A.D.D. impacted person is to understand that they are extremely capable of high level intelligence, incredible analytical and abstract thinking and may go places that your mind might have difficulty even comprehending. Understand that, if there is a comprehension problem it is not in their ability to comprehend, it is in the way the information is being presented. If they seem distracted, either the presenter has not conveyed the information in a way which is interesting and has not held their attention or they got it ten minutes ago and the presenter needs to get with the program and move on to something else.

The Intellectual Level:
Why the A.D.D. Impact is a gift

It is a gift because of the ability to comprehend, reason and expand intellectually more than we ever have before. Earlier, I made comparisons to working with a computer. Let us return to that analogy. This time, let us look at processors. The original computers had much slower processors than the ones we have today. As time progressed, they got faster and smaller, but only so fast and so small. Then there was a breakthrough and a different kind of processor came on to the scene. It worked differently. Adjustments needed to be made. We suddenly looked at things differently—different supports, set-ups and configurations. The world was astounded. There was dancing in the streets about the new technology, the new capacity and the new abilities.

So, let us look at the A.D.D. impacted person. They have a new way of processing. They need different support systems and configurations in order to work. The world should be dancing in the streets, not standing in the lines at the local pharmacies in fear of change. Imagine the possibilities.

Summary For The Intellectual Level

The more we know, the more we know what we do not know. Sound familiar? Many variations of this idea have existed over the centuries. We have not built foundations for children to grow upon. Instead, we have built four-sided prisons for our children-telling them what is possible and not possible, what they are capable or not capable of. We have always had those renegades who have blown through all the limitations. Now the number has just been dramatically increased. We have spent centuries building walls of right and wrong, black and white. An increased intellectual capacity will help us break through these limitations. An increased capacity might also allow us to recover from the damage we have done not only to each other but also to the earth and everything else that resides here.

What do you need to remember? It is not about a lack of capacity. It is not about an inability. It is about being different. Figure out your natural communication and thought styles. See if the ones you have are really the ones that are natural to you or are they survival or self-protection mechanisms. Then see what style of the A.D.D. intellectual impact most relates to what goes on inside your head. What tools and skills might help you harness all that great brainpower you are capable of using?

Chapter 5
Spiritual Body

The spiritual body is the place where we connect to our own Divine, to the Divine of others and to *the* Divine. It holds the memories of the places we have come from since the beginning of time. It is the place that holds what we came in to do, to be and become within this lifetime. And it is the place where we hold the knowledge or our own divinity.

The Spiritual body:
What has it been designed to do?

The spiritual body was created to help guide us to a greater understanding of the physical, emotional, intellectual and spiritual realms. It is the body that survives eternally, through the birth-death- rebirth process; a process we have been repeating for millennia as we evolve. It holds the experiences that we have gained through those lifetimes as well as the knowledge of which of those experiences are in or out of balance. In this body, we also have the understanding of our greater self, as well as the greater self of others. We understand our purpose in both the microcosms, of this lifetime, and the greater macrocosm, of our divine purpose.

Besides intellectual understanding, the spiritual body holds our unconditional love for others and ourselves. It also holds our ability for the channeling of Divine energy in order to facilitate healing. Depending on the amount of connection a person may have in a lifetime, they may channel Divine energy, their own personal energy, a combination of both or an alternating source of energies.

The spiritual body is also the place from where one can channel divine knowing. Depending on the amount of connection any one person may have in a lifetime, they may channel Divine knowing to help facilitate healing or they may access information from the collective unconscious or their higher self. On the other hand, they may channel knowing from someone else's higher self or read their mind and tell them what they want to hear! In some cases, they may be accessing a message or insight from someone who is disincarnate. Sometimes a person might do is just figure out what another person wants to hear or tell that person something so malleable that it can be twisted to fit anyone's life. This person is channeling what we call the P. T. Barnum energy of *"there is a sucker born every minute."* In case you have not figured it out, what I am trying to say is our spiritual and psychic gifts are also connected through the spiritual body.

The Spiritual body:
The box we have created for it

We have done a number of crazy things to our spiritual bodies; we have created numerous dysfunctional situations to house it. We have taken spirituality and made it exclusive, not inclusive. We have put spirituality outside of ourselves. We have instilled spirituality into objects, books, rituals, birthrights and/or perhaps even some physical attributes that may show up at birth or during someone's lifetime. We have held up examples of spirituality as a 'might means right' mentality. We have certainly, many times throughout history, looked to others for our spiritual connection. Oftentimes we bestow that honor upon those most gifted in speech. And sometimes they are in touch with the divine but just as often they are hate mongers, bigots, or simply self-righteous.

We have created religions and cults-whole cultures to give us definition, structure and rules to follow concerning how to access the spiritual. We are even told who the chosen ones are or through whom we need to access God. It is our spiritual selves that gets the credit and blame for billions of deaths, countless atrocities and endless streams of soul destroying, battery acid-laced judgments against our fellow beings. Often, there is very little spirituality in what we have done in the name of God.

The Spiritual Body: The A.D.D. impact

A greater connection to our spiritual selves is the impact that A.D.D. has when affecting the spiritual level. The people impacted on this level are more consciously aware of themselves as spiritual beings. They see themselves here for some kind of purpose and know that they are here to make the world a better place. When they are allowed to touch it, both children and adults will speak of knowing that they are here for a greater purpose. Here are some of the things that a few of my clients have shared with me:

A twelve-year-old male child upon asking him what was 'hurting' him in his life: "It hurts me to be human when I see what we have done, not only to each other, but to the planet itself. And I know I am here to make it better, but it hurts me to be human and see what we have done."

A thirteen-year-old male: "I know I have all this stuff, these gifts, that I am here to do something with. I just do not know how to get to them."

A nineteen year old male: "I cannot describe it, how I feel, but every time I see man do something destructive to the earth, it's like I feel the pain."

A forty-two year old woman: "I have always been so frustrated knowing I have all of these gifts to give the world and I just cannot seem to touch them enough to do it."

<u>*An eight-year-old male*</u>*: "I know I have to make the world a better place or soon there will not be an earth to be a better place."*

<u>*A twenty-seven year old woman*</u>*: "I am here to make the world a better place, I just wish people would stop trying to get in my way, and stop trying to limit me and medicate me because I do things differently. It's not my problem they do not understand."*

<u>*A nine-year old boy*</u>*: "I know I can have great power over people and I do not want to misuse it."*

I am not saying that non-A.D.D. people are spiritually unaware or not as spiritual. What I am saying is that the A.D.D. impacted people, as a group, seem to be more obviously and consciously aware of themselves as spiritual beings. Many of these comments have wisdom that one would expect from someone who had been consciously working on their path for some time, not someone who is eight or twelve or even nineteen years of age. Alongside this general awareness is a heightening of psychic/intuitive abilities. Like any individual who has been made uncomfortable with their own psychic abilities or has been 'pushed' into denying them, the A.D.D. impacted person might not be aware of these abilities. Once they are able to touch them and own them, however, look out! Empathy seems to be one psychic gift that is heightened somewhat with the majority of people I have worked with. Empathy is the ability to 'feel' what someone else is feeling and sometimes even 'take on' those feelings. This can leave the other person feeling better and the A.D.D. impacted person with the feelings to process through.

There are a number of other ways that the spiritual body might play out the A.D.D. impact, but those would be more so on a case to case basis. It boils down to an increase of awareness and an increase of abilities.

The Spiritual Body:
Managing The Gift

Managing the gift of the spiritually impacted A.D.D. person is by far the easiest of the four levels. It evolves around four basic concepts:

1.   *Help them learn how to shield and protect themselves.*
2.   *Assist them in developing their own spiritual abilities.*
3.   *Separate them from any limiting or judgmental concepts around spirituality.*
4.   *Support the person as a spiritual being.*

The last is the easiest of the four. If you are supporting someone who is being impacted by A.D.D., start by recognizing yourself as a spiritual being. See yourself as divinity on earth. For the impacted person, start an active exploration of a spiritual path. As you begin this process, remember that you redefine what spirituality can be. The same might hold true for many of the new things that will be introduced to you . . . not that this information will be right or wrong, just not applicable to you. Because of the increase of spiritual awareness, helping the A.D.D. impacted person to see himself or herself, as a spiritual being is not a difficult task once you can get through their feelings of isolation. All of this depends, of course, on how spirituality has been portrayed to them.

Help them learn how to shield and protect themselves

There are a number of different ways to protect and shield yourself so that you are not taking on other people's emotions or being sucked dry by other people. The book I would most recommend would be *Invisible Armor: Protecting Your Personal Energy* by Thomas Hensel. As long as there has been energy, there have been those that will dump the energy they do not want on whoever will take it and those that will suck dry any energy source they can access. You, as a person supporting an A.D.D. impacted person, need to learn about shielding and protection as well. This is to make sure that you are neither the one being sucked dry nor the one doing the sucking. Also, make sure that you are not taking on other people's stuff or putting your stuff onto other people.

More often than not, people are not aware of playing any of those roles. They feel the effect of playing the role, but they do not quite understand why they are feeling what they are feeling. So, someone may feel drained after spending time with another person but not be able to quite put their finger on why. Alternatively, they may have emotions whirling around in them and not know where they came from. On the other hand, one can also know that they feel good, energized or powerful after exchanges with some people and not know why.

Depending on the level of impact on the emotional body, these feelings can be quite skewed. An empath does not necessarily have to create an emotion to feel a feeling. Remember the earlier definition of the word emotion? Emotion is energy in motion and the energy is in motion as long as it has been catalyzed by an event. A feeling can be a sense of something. And a feeling can grow to the point where it can create an emotion, but it does not always *have* to create an emotion. So, the empath can take on a feeling, a vague sensation, or they can take on an emotion; therefore needing to process the emotion that has been taken on. Sometimes the emotion will go into the emotional body hold/drop pattern and sometimes it will circumvent it. This will happen especially if the feeling is a vague feeling. These vague feelings can be the way in which their intuitive may be speaking to them—throwing an additional consideration into the pot.

The isolation factor that often accompanies the A.D.D. impacted person works in their favor. This is because the isolation can act as a type of shielding and protection not a healthy kind, but a kind that will work. That is why it is important that, as the isolation gets broken through, a healthier type of shielding is in place. This will ensure that the person will not become overwhelmed.

Assist them in developing their own spiritual abilities

It is hard enough for anyone who has not been brought up in an open and supportive environment to start the journey of being open to his or her spiritual selves. Oftentimes, the A.D.D. impacted person has already felt different, like an outsider. Getting them to open up to their intuitive side can seem risky to them—just another way in which they will not fit in.

Around the age of four or five we, start getting messages to discard any evidence of our spiritual being, at least the spiritual being which is showing itself in esoteric ways. So if a child is expressing past life memories, seeing energy fields, talking to dead people or if they 'know' something they could not possibly know, then we start talking to them about 'growing up' or 'being a big boy or girl' and not making things up. We may also accuse them of lying. In some manner we communicate to them that what they are doing, sometimes even who they are, is wrong. We all know that children can be very imaginative, but we must be careful not to automatically dismiss everything that is not black and white by calling it 'imagination.' It is also making sure that you are not trying to dismiss or eliminate the behavior because it makes you, the adult, more uncomfortable or requires you to shift your perspective or stretch your comfort zones. It is often said that children are our greatest teachers, so let them be. For the A.D.D. impacted adult, encourage them to go out on the limb. Encourage them to read, take classes and find someone to work with who will help them discover and own themselves as spiritual beings.

Separate them from any limiting or judgmental concepts around spirituality

There are many kinds of religious belief systems, as well as cultural and social belief systems, that support and promote bigotry and encourage their followers to be judgmental. This person has been judged most of their cognitive lifetime. As soon as they obviously displayed 'differences', the judgement process began. It is easy for this person to become self-judgmental as well as judgmental of others. The last thing they need is any kind of encouragement that is going to more seriously batter their already battered self-esteem. Nor do they need to be taught to 'hide' or 'deflect' other's judgement of themselves by judging others first. Any or all combinations of judgment or hate mongering will add poison to an already toxified system.

The Spiritual Body:
Why the A.D.D. Impact is a gift

Being more aware of ourselves as divine pieces of God on earth is clearly a gift. To be more aware of the divinity of all things and feel more of the divinity in all things is clearly a gift, and having the ability to have two way communications with Spirit is a gift. To understand that we do not need anyone else's interpretation of God's messages is a gift. To be consciously be aware of a commitment to be here in order to make the world a better place, from Spirit's perspective, not any one group or belief system, is a gift. The list of gifts goes on. In fact, why not stop for a moment and think up a few for yourself? It can be a most enlightening and rewarding experience.

Summary For The Spiritual Level

As a person impacted with A.D.D., no matter how hard you try to run away from it, cover it up or deny it, you are intimately tied up with the Earth. You are also intimately entwined with all things on Earth and the future towards which we are all heading—with or without a planet to stand upon when we get there. You may have been lucky enough to have had support systems that promoted your unique spiritual being or this may have been another area where you were different, ostracized and just given another reason to become and stay isolated. The words to you are, "Yes, you are different. Big deal! Everybody is and different is okay." Knowing or feeling or doing things that most of the people you grew up with either would not or could not do does not mean you should not or that it is wrong. Find your spiritual self and a loving, compassionate, divine, and nonjudgmental higher being and you will be just fine.

Chapter 6
Anxiety, Isolation, Shame & Fear

The factors of anxiety, isolation, shame and fear can play out in many different ways. The first understanding needed here in order to make a difference in the life of the A.D.D. impacted person is that they are all playing out in varying degrees. Depending on the personality, upbringing, and support or lack thereof these factors will play out differently. Let us first examine how and why they are caused. Instead of giving specific examples for each, I am going to follow example to highlight anxiety, isolation, shame and fear.

Let us call our child Chris. Between the ages of three and four, Chris begins to realize that he is different than the other children around him. He is even different than the expectations that his parents have of him. He does not seem to respond the way they expect him to respond. They may question his responses. They may question why he is not as 'happy' as he should be about some experience. He feels happy, but he is not as outwardly happy as expected. He tends to have a harder time sleeping and is often wound up to the point that he fidgets. His sense of curiosity is overwhelming. He understands more than he has developed the vocabulary to express and, when not being driven by all this energy, he can be quite content lost in his own little world. It is starting dawn on our little Chris, how different he is, although he may be well on the way to five before he really begins to put it all together. Let us not forget that Chris is an extremely bright and sensitive child—not sensitive to criticism (though he may be), but sensitive to energy. By the time Chris moves from four to five, he definitely notices any anxiety within the household. Chris has also had more and more interaction with other children and sees for himself the differences. Though he may not quite be sure yet that they are bad, these differences sure do not look good.

Chris then begins developing the intellectual emotional body that we talked about in chapter three. He knows that the people around him are starting to become concerned and he definitely does not want to be different in a bad way. He starts to feel like he has something he needs to keep hidden, something he must learn to control. His need to be active is now being called hyperactive and his lack of emotions are being referred to as odd, even though he does have emotions and they seem wild and uncontrolled when they come. He might have even heard himself discussed as a problem or overheard that he might need to go see a doctor to see what is wrong with him. Depending when he begins school or preschool, these issues become more pro-nounced.

By this point, Chris has learned shame and fear. The more he interacts with a world where he does not fit in, the more Chris also starts dealing with anxiety-the anxiety that he is going to do something which will make him stand out in a bad way. He begins to fear that his parents will stop loving him. He wonders why he is such a 'bad' child and the more he feels like no one understands him, the more he feels isolated. He feels that no one really under-stands what is going on inside of him and if they knew, then they would really stop loving him.

Our little Chris, depending on the parents, the school system and other environmental factors, finally comes to the inevitable conclusion that he is defective, disabled, undesirable and even unlovable. There are many paths that Chris can take with that information, but they all unfold from the misconception that he is a problem and is somehow bad or wrong.

If you think that telling the child you love him will make him feel lovable, you will find that you are wrong more often than not. I have worked with many young adult children whose parents tell them that they love them. But because they have all these other factors and fears playing out, once I have broken through the isolation I hear over and over again: "Do not tell my parents about how bad I am because they will not love me anymore." How can you be lovable when everyone has convinced you that you are defective and broken? To compound the issue, these other people do not understand what is going on inside of the A.D.D. impacted individual because not even they understand it. So how do you help these people?

Here is a list for the parent to help your child avoid that trap, or help them get out of it if they have already started the descent. Following that is a list for the A.D.D. impacted adult of how to help themselves break out of any of the anxiety, isolation, shame and/or fear that they may still be experiencing.

Helping Your Child with Anxiety, Isolation, Shame & Fear

1. Begin talking to your child at an early age about how differences are not only acceptable but that they are a good thing.
2. As you see them struggle with emotions, explain how people deal with emotions differently and try to help them understand how their emotional body works.
3. Figure out, as best you can, how all their different bodies work and begin working with your child to understand the process.
4. Avoid judgmental and/or comparison comments, even if they are in your child's favor.
5. When your child is confronted with 'better than/ worse than' comments, work with them to understand that being better at something does not

indicate that the person is better—just better at a specific activity or task and that we all have things we are better at.

6. When you have to use terms always use terms like diff-ability, not disability. Stress to your child that they learn differently, they feel differently and even their 'energy levels' are different. And that all of these things, are just as natural, they just do not occur as often, so you meet fewer people with them.

7. Listen carefully. Be aware of where your children are getting negative feedback about who they are. Do not be afraid to stand up for your child, especially around issues to do with the school system.

8. Many things can exacerbate some of the normal differences of the A.D.D. impacted child. These need to be addressed before some of the other recommendations will really begin to help. These things include diet, use of supplements, monitoring environment and use of meditating and centering techniques.

9. Never let anyone bully you or your child into using medications. Make sure you have fully exhausted and truly utilized a holistic approach to help your child embrace his/her gifts.

10. Always refer to A.D.D. as a gift and help your child understand that it is a gift.

11. Be willing to stretch your comfort zones and utilize resources other than those with which you may be familiar. Remember that it is your child's well being at stake, so stretch and do it for them.

The following are some of the things that I suggest for the A.D.D. impacted adult to help with any leftover anxiety, isolation, shame and fear, or any side effects that were created. These things also help with any protective mechanisms or survival skills that the person developed, things that were once necessary but are now no longer needed or healthy.

Helping Yourself with Anxiety, Isolation, Shame & Fear

1. At the very least, accept that these things have existed in your life even if they are no longer existent.
2. Identify and begin working with your *intellectual-emotional* body as well as your *emotional* body.
3. Identify how you have played out these different things within your own life.
4. Begin the approach of holistically evaluating your life. Keep in mind the things you have learned through reading this book.
5. Start using affirmations to help rewrite some of the negative self-belief systems that you have created.
6. As you begin to feel more positive about yourself, go back and re-evaluate your childhood with the new insights and understandings.
7. Monitor your language for verbiage that is limited, counter-productive or expressions of low self-esteem or self-worth. Catch yourself using those words and be willing to correct yourself aloud, even if it is mid-sentence. This means catching yourself referring to being stupid or disabled, or that not as much can be expected from you because you are A.D.D.
8. Begin work on your own spiritual path and the self-discovery of yourself as a spiritual being. Be willing to stretch your comfort zones.

9. Work with someone who is in agreement with the fact that your A.D.D. is a gift, not something to be fixed or covered up with drugs.

10. Share your discoveries with your support systems and ask them to help your healing process.

These lists are neither the 'be all' nor the 'end all.' They are merely helpers along the way. They can, upon use, help with many more issues beyond those specifically related to the A.D.D. impact.

Chapter 7
For The Children

Throughout most of the book, I have tried to frame things in a context for both adults and children impacted with A.D.D. In this chapter, I am going to share some things for the parents and adult caretakers about how to help their children and what to be aware of about their children and their environment.

I will list a set of steps that I would encourage parents to take in order to best ensure the success of their child in not only managing the gift of A.D.D., in becoming all that they are capable of becoming. These are also steps to help alleviate the scarring that many children and adults have developed because of the ignorance and prejudice surrounding A.D.D. The following is a list of suggestions that I will then explain in greater detail:

Steps To Help Your Child

1. Never assume that your child has A.D.D. because someone thinks or tells you that that he/she does.

2. Do a checklist on your child to eliminate outside factors that could be giving the appearance of A.D.D.

3.   If your child is impacted by A.D.D., explain to your child and all your child's support systems how you see A.D.D. and how it is to be handled.

4.   As much as possible, limit unsupervised visits with your child by anyone who creates a victim mentality or who believes that your child is disabled or has a mental or behavioral problem.

5.   Begin, as early as possible, creating an organized and structured environment for your child and teach them to be organized and structured.

6.   If a parent cannot stay home during the child's early years through the adolescent years, then choose a single supportive adult over a group setting.

7.   Choose the educational settings with great care and be prepared to be a watchdog.

8.   Listen carefully to your child. They will tell you what they need. They will also tell you if they are being disempowered and if so, by whom.

9.   Be prepared to coach your child on how to handle the adults around them, especially those who want to make them disabled, dismiss them 'because they are disabled' or are pushing to medicate them.

10. Know your rights and never assume that someone else's idea of 'in the best interest of your child' is actually in *your* child's best interest. Or that the school system is going to educate you or help you stand up for your rights if you do not know them.

11. Neither entitling nor enabling your child helps them with making their way in the world or managing their A.D.D.

12.   Be willing to fight for your child.

If only villains always wore black and the good people always wore white, the world would be such an easier place to live in. In the case of your child, everybody sees themselves in the white clothes and, more often than not, will see people who disagree with their methods in the black. Although you are the one who will ultimately make the decisions, make sure you listen to your child and involve them every step of the way. When I watched the 'Merrow Report' special on A.D.D., it amazed me how often kids beg, plead, promise and threaten their parents to not put them on drugs- only to be ignored. From the 'Merrow Report' here are some words from one child who wrote an article for his school newspaper:

"Schools don't like extremists who like to think and question. They are the dreamers. That doesn't mean that they are wrong. They just don't fit the norm, so they are labeled and damned, labeled as A.D.D. (Attention Deficit Disorder).

So the doctors dope us up with Ritalin and control our minds with low doses of speed . . . Ritalin does not help me learn; it simply lowers my mind down between the selected lines in which we are taught. Who's going to get further in life, the schmo with the same textbook answers and ideas, or the "A.D.D. kid" who can offer idea that have never been thought of or a new perspective on something? I truly look forward to the day when Ritalin isn't an answer. To the day when every student is labeled "learner."

Matt Scherbel was 14 and in the eight grade at Thomas Pyle Middle School in Bethesda, MD when he wrote this for his school newspaper, "The Pyle Print."

This is especially disheartening when not every avenue has been explored and all the consultants in the matter are drug therapy biased. There is truth in the old adage, "From the mouths of babes . . ." [1]

---

[1] The Merrow Report *Attention Deficit Disorder: A Dubious Diagnosis?* 588 Broadway Suite 510 New York, NY 10012 _Phone:_ 212.941.8060 _Fax:_ 212.941.8068 _Homepage:_ www.pbs.org/merrow E-Mail: merrow@pbs.org.

Never assume that your child has A.D.D. because someone thinks or tells you that that he/she does.

A.D.D. has become a hot topic and a popular diagnosis. Many times, the actual contact with medically or psychologically trained individuals is extremely limited. There are more initial diagnoses coming from the school than the doctor and the 'official' diagnosis is heavily based on the school's recommendation and input. I want to clearly state here that I am not making the school system or the teachers 'the bad guys.' However, I do see, from research, first hand reports and what I have witnessed, that classroom size, staffing, support and view of the administration, as well as the competency of the teachers can create situations where the classroom itself could give a child many of the symptoms associated with A.D.D. If you are approached by a teacher, school counselor or school administrator with the idea that your child has A.D.D. and would do better if it were under control (i.e. drug 'em), take a deep breath and remember that the diagnosis is still very much up for grabs.

Do a checklist on your child to eliminate outside factors that could be giving the appearance of A.D.D.

Many factors can look like 'symptoms' of A.D.D. Here are a few which you might like to check, even before you seek outside professional help:

Diet
Allergies
Illness
Accidents
Emotional traumas
Exposure to toxic products
Unsettled energies at home
Unsettled energies at school

See if you can trace back to where there have been any

personality changes or any sudden attitude or outlook changes. Is the child in front of you at this moment the same child who stood in front of you last week, last month, last year? The information I have received has never given any indication that A.D.D. suddenly 'appears' one day. If your child was mellow, laid-back and go-with-the-flow at the age of four and at five is a wild child onto whom the system wants to push the A.D.D. cure-all pills, you are barking up the wrong tree.

If you really hope to examine the possibilities of outside influences giving your child the appearances of being impacted by A.D.D., then I would recommend *The Hyperactivity Hoax* by Sydney Walker III, MD[2]. He is very good at illuminating the alternative things that can look like hyperactivity. I do not agree with his all-too-predictable conclusion (if your child is impacted by A.D.D./A.D.H.D., then medicate them), but it is still an informative read.

If your child is impacted by A.D.D., explain to your child and all your child's support systems how you see A.D.D. and how it is to be handled.

You can set the tone and help shape the experience your child has with by A.D.D. It is a negative experience for many children. Establish with your child that he or she is not *disabled* (a term that indicates a lesser capacity), but that they have a *diff-ability*—they learn differently, not to a lesser degree. It is then important that all of your child's support systems reinforce that concept. It does not take much for your child's self-worth and self-esteem to become compromised.

As much as possible, limit unsupervised visits with your child by anyone who creates a victim mentality or who believes that your child is disabled or has a mental or behavioral problem.

First, remember that there is no such thing as a child who brings no problems or no challenges. We have children so that

---

[2] Walker, Sydney, MD *The Hyperactivity Hoax,* St. Martin's Press, Dec. 1998

they can bring problems and challenges. It is part of our growth experience. But there may be those around you who feel that you are in denial or are being unrealistic. And there may be around you those who will do their best to *make* your child disabled. There is nothing more disabling than a child who is robbed of their confidence, self-worth and self-esteem. These people will go over the line of supporting your child's differences to that of enabling them to become victims of their A.D.D. Part of your job in parenting this child is to protect your child from these influences. For many people, it may be a warm up for setting and enforcing boundaries around your child. You might as well get used to this because, in this social and educational climate, you could easily need to do this a great deal. For those parents who never learned to set and enforce their own boundaries, now you know why you gave birth to this gifted child.

Begin, as early as possible, creating an organized and structured environment for your child, and teach them to be organized and structured.

As we discussed in earlier chapters, organizational tools are very important for the person impacted with A.D.D. Developing those skills and tools for yourself and role modeling them to your child can prevent many problems. Explain the 'why' and 'wherefore' to the child to help them become willing to participate in organizing themselves. Structure is also important. It is important to any child, but particularly to your child. Children whose A.D.D. impacts them only mildly on the physical level often end up not 'acting out' or getting 'diagnosed' until they are in junior high school. This is because grade school tends to have more structure and less self-responsibility and choice making factors. And these children need more guidance in developing those areas. So, unless the child has been taught the tools and skills to create their own structure and organization, they start to have meltdowns in junior high school. The pressure is up and the skill level is not such that they can cope. Peer pressure is also up and puberty explodes onto the scene.

If a parent cannot stay home during the child's early years through the adolescent years, then choose a single supportive adult over a group setting.

Following this path eliminates the need to make sure that other people are taking the same approach or following the same structures and organizational tools that you have created. It also cuts down on the possibility of having to 'correct' any misperceptions that your child would pick up that he/she is disabled, a problem or handicapped. The sooner the child is exposed to an ongoing peer group, the quicker he or she will be exposed to other people's perceptions of them and their 'condition'. A child who is instilled with confidence, self-esteem and self-worth by the time they are five or six will have a strong base from which to draw when they are integrated with the world at large, particularly school. But if they start to worry about being different or get labeled or declared handicapped or disabled at three or four, they will take that into their social and educational situations, possibly for the rest of their lives. Labels are hard to lose internal labels are the worst. Also, that extra time between three and six are years in which the child can begin to get better at managing their own gift. I am not advocating isolation here. In fact, I am trying to prevent it. Do not eliminate all social contact, just not the social contact that is in a regular pre-school situation.

If you are a parent with a three or four-year-old and you have been told your child is A.D.D. and you have decided that it is a likely probability, then you probably have your child in some kind of pre-school. If that is true, pull that child out if possible. If a parent cannot be present for the majority of the child's time, then find one other constant adult who understands your child's needs at this time or find one who is willing to be educated to the way in which you want your child's needs addressed.

Choose the educational settings with great care and be prepared to be a watchdog.

I am a big advocate for private education or home schooling. This comes from knowing what it takes to meet the needs of your child. Remember that all children have a variety of needs.

The school system accommodates some of the needs for most of the children. It has a limited list of needs for which it is willing to provide, often only when forced. It will do in the way, which is most expedient and will best fit into the system as it has been created. When the school does create a program, for your child, that program will most often reflect how the system perceives your child's conditions and needs rather than what you want done for your child. There is very little room for your perception of the child's condition and needs, unless they fit into the system. Like any other state or government system, the school system will often be good only if you make it accountable.

Recently, while in a meeting, an assistant superintendent of schools was trying to explain to me how the school system was set up on the assembly line, factory model. He explained that the school system was set up for the average child and would not accommodate those children who were on either side of the "conveyer belt." That belt prepared them to be ready for the real world and children who could not make it in the school system and adjust to the belt were not likely to make it in the world. When I asked him about the concept of the children's happiness he "reminded" me that life was not about being happy; it was about fitting in and getting by. These concepts in many ways have filtered into the modern workplace as well. The room for difference is small, tolerance little and cost high

Listen carefully to your child. They will tell you what they need. They will also tell you if they are being disempowered and, if so, by whom.

If your child starts asking questions about their 'differences' or why other kids are medicated or even why are they treated differently, sit down, give them your full attention and listen to what they are saying. Even by what they say and how they are saying it, or by the questions they ask, you will get insight as to where they are hearing the comments. If not, then ask. In responding, do not invalidate what your child has been hearing. Address it, and explain to them, in a language that they can understand, why they might think that or where that kind of thinking comes from. Do this in a positive way. Among other things, you will be teaching your child critical thinking skills. You will also not be role modeling the kind of judgement that is creating pain in their life.

Be prepared to coach your child on how to handle the adults around them, especially those who want to make them disabled, dismiss them "because they are disabled" or are pushing to medicate them.

By teaching your child how to see him/herself, think through what others are telling them with discernment and keep their self-esteem in place, you have already won half this battle. You now need to teach them how they need to 'educate' other people who do not understand what their condition is and why it is a gift. They need to learn to do this in a way that is polite, yet firm. You, the parent, need to be willing to support your child in this role.

Know your rights and never assume that someone else's idea of 'in the best interest of your child' is actually in your child's best interest. Or that the school system is going to educate you or help you stand up for your rights if you do not know them.

'Adversarial' is often the best word for the relationship between administration and parents when you want something different other than what they are willing to do for your child's diagnosis. If this were just my observation or that of the parents I have dealt with, I might hesitate putting that statement in this book. However, a number of other sources come to the same conclusion. When you hear it from primary sources, hear it from reported sources and witness it yourself, then you have to start giving it some validity. I am not saying that all school systems are going to do the minimum of what is required or that all school systems will resist anything out of their normal approach. What I am saying is to be prepared. You may have thus far had nothing but positive experiences with your school system. If you have yet to offer an alternative to something they want to do, however, you may be in for a big surprise. At the end of this chapter, I have an appendix, which includes two handouts that I give in my workshop. One is a sheet titled 'Do You Know You Have A Right To . . .' and the other is a list of additional resources.

Neither entitling nor enabling your child helps them with making their way in the world or managing their A.D.D.

For some children, they learn at an early age how to manipulate situations to their best advantage. I have more than once heard a child give a very 'adult' quote about how they cannot or should not be expected to do something because they have A.D.D. I am the first one to say that there are considerations that need to be given to the children who are impacted with A.D.D. in order for them to succeed. Nevertheless, do not teach or allow your child to use it as a universal excuse for anything they do not want to do or anything that they have done for which any other child would have been held accountable. These children are very bright and they will sense if you feel guilty or will quickly pick up on you making excuses for them and they will use it. So make sure that you hold your child accountable, make consequences clear to them, and follow through. Often I recommend that as soon as a child is old enough they be allowed to co-create the consequences of doing or not doing something. Insist they participate and they will have more ownership.

Be willing to fight for your child.

Let me share a few stories to illustrate why I say, "Be prepared to fight."

> *One woman I worked with in Virginia, when trying to work with school officials about her son and his needs, was told the only problem was that the boy had a mother who did not know how to discipline him. Until he had a father or until she learned to discipline him, it was better that they continue to flunk him. His issue was not behavior; it was*

homework.

*****

*In one meeting I attended, the teachers and guidance
counselor were very nice. We all suspected that the child in
question was impacted with A.D.D., and that the child was
more than capable and very bright. We (the mother and I)
expressed that we were not interested in diagnosing, labeling
or medicating the child. They all noted an improvement
with the child since he had been working with me.*

*Unfortunately, when we asked that the teachers be
willing to make a note in a log that would go home to the
mother so she could help him organize homework and
projects, we were refused. Unless we were willing to get
something 'official' then there was nothing 'extra' they were
willing to do. The guidance counselor explained that the
teachers did not have the time to do that unless it was
mandated by an IEP (Individual Education Plan) that
would be created for a child with the proper diagnosis.
When I asked them if they had other children for whom
this service was provided, the answer was, "Yes . . . because
they have to."*

*****

*Another parent had a child who was 'official' in his
A.D.D. diagnosis and his reputation as a 'trouble kid'
preceded him. Whenever she pushed, his accommodations
were met, but often with malice. This child was given extra
time for tests, but when the teacher forgot (often) and was
asked by the child that he be given the time, the child was
humiliated in front of the class for asking. Whenever
anything happened and he was anywhere nearby, it was
assumed he was involved even if there was no evidence.
When this child told the teacher once, after a conversation
with me, that he had a diff-ability and that it was the
school that was disabled in teaching him, they tried to*

punish him and did not follow through only because of the mother's intervention. Two things changed this eroding situation. The first was sending him to a private summer camp which specialized in working with A.D.D. impacted children. They brought him up to his grade level and helped him start to develop the skills that he needed. The second thing that changed the situation was his mother getting a lawyer. Unfortunately, I have had to make both of these recommendations all too often.

*****

Another single parent had been going through IEPs for her son over the last several years. It was not until she worked with me that she realized that she disagreed with the education plans. In the team meeting, she was given the assessment of her child, was told what they were going to do for him and about him and asked if she had any questions. She was then given the paper and told to sign it and that they would meet again next year. She signed it because she did not know that she had a right to disagree and nobody at that meeting was going to tell her any differently.

I am not saying that every person who wants something other than what a school system wants is going to have to fight for it. However, being prepared to fight for your child could save you and your child a great deal of heartache and pain later.

Do You Know You Have A Right To . . .

- . . . request a Pupil Evaluation Team (P.E.T.) meeting to discuss possible testing and voice concerns which any team member(which you are) may have.

- . . . bring anyone to the meeting.

- . . . written Prior Notice of a P.E.T meeting, which includes the purpose, time, location and participants.

- . . . a team meeting scheduled at a time and place convenient for you.

- . . . participate in all meetings relative to evaluation, eligibility(coding), IEP(individual educational plan), and placement.

- . . . tape record any meeting unless the school district has a valid written school board policy prohibiting this(note: even if the district has such a policy you may still be able to tape record a meeting in certain situations under the Family Educational Rights and Privacy Act).

- . . . a copy of your rights, which you should accept and date.

- . . . receive a copy of the minutes if, they were recorded.

- . . . revise the minutes if they do not reflect your perceptions of the meeting. Write down what you believe was discussed or decided and send a copy to school to be included in your child's file.

- . . . withhold your permission. No evaluation or testing for special needs can be done without your permission and you can withdraw your permission at any time.

- ... request assessments from independent educational evalua-
tors such as audiologists, psychologists, psychiatrists, neurolo-
gists, physical and/ or occupational therapists, etc. who are not
employed by the school system.

- ... receive reports of any assessments that are done.

- ... know that there are timelines that the school must follow.
These differ from state to state.

- ... know that an IEP must be reviewed at least once a year.

- ... sign or not sign the IEP. Never sign the IEP at the
meeting.

- ... file for mediation or a due process hearing if you disagree
with an IEP, placement or other team decision.

- ... know that your child is covered under section 504 of the
Rehabilitation Act of 1973 which is a civil rights law whether
he/she is on an IEP plan or a 504 plan.

- ... add relevant comments, information or other written
materials to the student record.

- ... request that information be changed or taken out of the
student record. If the school refuses, you have the right to
have a hearing on this.

- ... file a complaint with the Office for Civil Rights if you feel
your child's civil rights have been violated.

Additional Resources

1. *Family Education Network*
    Their website is:
    familyeducation.com/topic/front/0,1156,1-2426,00.html
    This is a great resource with many links.

2. *ADD Warehouse*
    Phone: (800) 233-9273.
    Call and ask for their catalog.

3. *C.H.A.D.D.*
    www.chadd.org
    Much information with many links.

4. *One Add Place*
    www.greatconnect.com/oneaddplace.htm
    Much information with many links.

5. *Talking Back to Ritalin* by Peter Briggin
    www.breggin.com
    Other links information about Ritalin.

6. *Technical Assistance Alliance for Parent Centers*
    Their website is *www.taalliance.org*
    If you click on "WebLinks and Resources" you
    will see Parent Training and Information Centers.
    There is a Center in every state. These Centers are
    valuable resources for parents. They provide
    information about special education rules and
    regulations specific to the state they are in. Ask
    about any publications they have.

Chapter 8
For The Adults

As you may recall, I began this A.D.D. work in a session with a couple doing spiritually based marriage coaching and counseling. For adults, the challenges of being impacted with A.D.D. are both the same and different than for children. In this chapter, I discuss those things that apply to the adults and I will offer insight for their support systems.

I have broken this chapter into two categories: *Relationships* and *Career*. Before we look at these categories, there are a few things I would like to clarify. In any of the recommendations or observations that I share, remember that, like any other group, people within the A.D.D. impacted group will have more individual differences than similarities. Things like basic personality, upbringing, gender and where an individual is within their life will greatly influence how to play out these suggestions and insights. So if a trait or an insight does not quite seem to fit, pull back and look at the essences/gift of the message and how you might play it out within the specifics of your life. We have all developed self-protection mechanisms and survival skills that have helped us through life up to this point. Oftentimes, the greatest challenge in dealing with adults in my practice is the creative ways in which they have learned to play out what they have perceived as their shortcomings or liabilities when it comes to A.D.D. Another challenge has been dealing with the ways in which they survived and/or how others around them have dealt with A.D.D.

Relationships

Relationships, intimate and otherwise, have their unique challenges for the A.D.D. person. First, they must deal with any *isolation* that has been created. Second, they must deal with the unpredictability of *emotional release*. Third, they must deal with problems with their *attention span*. Fourth, they must deal with *making good choices* and *unexpected changes*. Fifth, they must deal with *memory* issues. Finally, they must deal with *physical energy level* issues.

Isolation

Isolation can play out in many different ways. I have seen it through shy, shutdown and isolated behavior. I have also seen it play out through the actions of being very pleasing. This person will do anything for anybody, allow themselves to be taken advantage of or will do anything to be liked. I also have seen it play out through being very judgmental, arrogant and condescending. They tend to point out other people's faults, focus very much on action and 'right versus wrong' or find somewhere else for the spotlight to be focused on by making themselves the keeper of the spotlight. Then there is the play out through defensiveness and the 'no one understands me' approach to life. This follows right on to the 'bad boy/girl,' the 'nothing I ever do is going to be right, so I might as well be good at being as bad as possible' syndrome. These seem like a variety of different masks, but they all accomplish the same thing: keeping other people away from finding the true person. This is often the play out of a person who feels like they are defective or broken.

Trusting and intimate sharing come slowly. For the A.D.D. individual, figuring out how to repair their self-esteem and coming to a place of true understanding about the gift of who they are provide the first steps in being able to explore themselves. This will then alleviate the need for distance. The self-understanding also aids in the creation of an environment that feels safer and allows the sharing. In order to get intimacy needs met, it is not uncommon for the A.D.D. person to share small bits and pieces of themselves with different people. It feels safer. For the support person, I would encourage you to allow the A.D.D. person to share. Accept what they share without pushing. Ask questions and become aware of how they are impacted with A.D.D. and how that affects them.

Emotional Releases

The adult impacted with A.D.D. needs to start by learning how to separate the intellectual emotional body from the true emotional body. If you are not sure how to do that, begin by trying to remember that time when you started to realize or notice what kind of emotions you were supposed to have and then started making sure that you had them. Then begin becoming aware of the emotions your have and see if you can figure out where your response really originates. I understand that this is neither an easy or simple process. You may need an outside person to help you do it. If you choose to work with a professional, make sure that they are philosophically harmonious with this approach to working with A.D.D.

Next, begin doing the emotional coffee breaks. If you are not sure how often to do them, then track when drops seem to happen. Measure the time in between them and divide that by two. Start by doing the coffee breaks that often. If this does not seem to eliminate the drops, then divide the original time by three and try that. If there is a great deal of unexpected stress and trauma going on in your life, you could be tripping your drop pattern more often. So, do more breaks . . . they will not hurt you.

For the support person, look for cycles. See if you can determine when they are starting to build up to a release. Encourage them to take their 'coffee break.' Encourage them to not have to 'put on' emotions because that is what is expected of them.

Finally, support them in following through on whatever actions they need to take when they do a coffee break.

Depending on your relationship with this person, their age, stage of life and upbringing, you may be dealing with an addiction problem or someone who is a rageaholic. You, the support person, must also set boundaries and be willing to do joint work with someone who can help both you and the A.D.D. person in your life. Do not take on the role of parent, spouse or friend and try to be therapist as well. Have a third party. So, if you are trying to figure out the drop pattern for someone in your life or yourself try this:

- Keep track for one week of when your emotional *drops* or crashes happen.
- Do they seem to be to be regular—such as once a day, twice a day, once every other day.
- Or do they seem to come in groups, a *drop* followed closely by one or two more drops, then a longer break before the next break.
- If you have a simple regular pattern then take the longest time between *drops* and divide it by two. Thus, the longest break is four hours then every two hours you should try to do an emotional coffee break.
- If your *drops* come in groups than still take the longest time between drops to calculate the best time to do emotional coffee breaks but in this case if a drop does occur do not try to start doing coffee breaks until the 'group' is done. So if the drop groups seem to happen once a day then twice a day you should do a coffee break and if you do have a drop then wait until the 'aftershocks' happen before you calculate the time to do the next coffee break.

Attention Span

Well, it is called *Attention Deficit Disorder*. Of course, there are likely to be some attention span issues in relationship, but you may be surprised at how those issues play out. Let us start with relationships in general.

Keep in mind that most individuals impacted with A.D.D. tend to hyperfocus. Therefore, when a new and interesting person comes into this individual's attention, they can make that person the thing on which they hyperfocus. It will depend on how much of a people person they are and how interesting the new person is compared to the other things going on in their world at the time. Whether friend or new romance, if you are the lucky one on whom they hyperfocus, be ready . . . be very ready. You will feel like the most interesting and desirable person in the world. Also, be ready for the time when the next interest comes along, because it is a wonderful pedestal but a tough fall. This does not mean you are history. It means that something more interesting has come into focus and the A.D.D. person will be back. The question is, "Will you be there?" If you are, you could easily get to breathe that rarified air again. However, if you want to stay in this person's life, you had better learn to fly or bounce well.

Regardless of the type of relationship, we are not talking about either loyalty or fidelity. For you, the A.D.D. individual, try to not make too many promises that you cannot keep and try to be as honest as you can with both yourself and the people in your life about your 'hyperfocusing.' For you, the support system, enjoy them when they are there and present. Keep your own life going and make it interesting. Always look at them as a wonderful addition, not the center. That is, of course, unless you are addicted to roller coaster rides.

I contemplated different places to touch upon this issue and finally decided that here was as good as any place to discuss the sex issue. I knew it needed to be under relationships, but did it need a whole separate category or would it be better under the physical energy area? When everything was said and done, if you, the A.D.D. individual is going to be impacted in the sexual area of your life the issue (more often than not) will be around your attention span. A new person, a new body, a new style—these will most likely keep your attention. New likes and dislikes, even some new ways will keep your attention. If something becomes the least bit predictable, the mind can easily wander and it is not even that it wanders to someone else or some sexual fantasy. It might tackle some problem you were having at work, a solution for the computer game that has you stumped or something that you forgot to do before you came to bed. Unpredictability and variety are certainly the remedy here. In addition, adjusting to the idea of an unpredictable sex life will help.

You, the partner, need to keep up your end of the bargain. Keep it interesting, a little off-putting and definitely unpredictable. Be contented with a sex drive that will definitely play out against the backdrop of what other areas of your partner's life are demanding hyperfocus, willingly or otherwise. For you, the partner, this arena can play out like the roller coaster ride. If your A.D.D. partner is a strong sexual being, then they will likely bring that hyperfocus into the bedroom and, for as long as it lasts, it could easily be the best you ever had. But when the hyperfocus wears off, you start wondering if they are cheating on you! All that sexual energy had to go somewhere, right? Well, sexual energy can easily be transmuted into all the other types of excess energy in your partner's life, whether it plays out as creative energy, mental energy, physical energy or even spiritual energy. There are plenty of places for it to go.

Making Good Choices and Unexpected Changes

This issue will definitely be affected by personality, stage of life and a number of other factors, so the first thing for you, the individual with A.D.D., is to classify how you play out changes and choices. Some people go with the flow. They forget all the commitments, promises and things that need to be done as soon as someone says, "Let's go do…" For other people a "I need you to do this for me today" creates stress. Others just will not do anything spontaneous. What I have discovered among some of my adults, even the ones who did not come to the awareness of being impacted by A.D.D. until they were adults, was that their survival skills came in the form of rigidity. When you are confronted with a sudden choice or change of plan do you shut down, get angry, become irresponsible or get rigid? Whatever the pattern, be willing to recognize it for what it is—a pattern, a survival skill, something that is probably going to cause you problems or, at the very least, stress and frustration.

Whatever your pattern, when a sudden change or choice comes, stop and do nothing for a moment. Take out your 'things to do' list and prioritize what makes the most sense according to what other commitments or deadlines do you have today and what is most attractive to you. Then make a decision. For you, the support system, do not tease and cajole or show some intense emotions. Rather, help them organize your suggestion or idea. If you do need them to do something, whenever possible, give the idea to them the evening before so that it can be incorporated. Do not throw something at them and tell them it needs to be done as soon as possible and rush off.

I once saw a coffee cup that said, *"Lack of planning on your part does not constitute an emergency on my part."* Avoid emergencies when possible and remember that what might be easy for you to fit in can ruin their day (and yours).

Memory

There are two issues within the memory issue. Let's look at your memory like the one in your computer. Its like an over-sized filing cabinet. So, the first issue is one of access. The problem with access derives from the amount of activity in the A.D.D. brain when information arrives. Instead of finding the right or best folder in which to file the information, it becomes stuck in whatever folder was open when you received the information—even if that folder has nothing to do with what the information is about. When it comes time to access it, it is diffi-cult because you do not know where it is.

The second issue occurs when the A.D.D. person receives information, which is not of interest to them. That information goes in under the temporary files category with a constant empty-ing of the recycling bin. When it comes time to find it, it is not there. You simply do not remember what does not interest you. The issue with remembering to do things is like copying to the clipboard; everything new replaces whatever was on it just before. So you ask them to do something and on the way to do it five new things pop into the brain and each is copied to the clipboard. Guess what happens when they get to wherever it was you sent them—they are truly and sincerely clueless as what you wanted them to do.

For you, the A.D.D. individual, make lists and get it in writing. If someone tells you something that needs to be done on the fly, tell him or her that if they do not write it down, it will not be done. Keep a little notebook on you at all times and use it to keep track of thoughts, ideas, things that need to be done and/or even things you need to tell people to do. Make sure you go through the little book and transfer everything you can onto one of your other lists and take care of what you can every night.

For you, the support system, when you know that the A.D.D. person is physically present but not wholly 'there,' and you need them to really hear something, make sure you get their attention. Have them repeat it after you. Engage them in conversation about it. Then write it down and give it to them. Try to not get upset on the occasions that it still does not register. Make it your responsibility to either insure that they write it down or write it down yourself and give it to them, placing it somewhere where they will see it and not have to search for it.

Physical Energy Level

Depending how you are affected on the physical level, do not expect any one person to keep up with you. Plan things every day that will help you to utilize all that energy and remember that something that simulates movement can sometimes be as effective. Another trick is to combine things: spend time with people while walking, running or working out, do a moving meditation, read a book on the treadmill or try book tapes—anything that will allow you to use your energy while focusing on something else. Pick different people with whom you are trying to maintain relationships and do different things with different people so that you do not wear out any one person. Sometimes just driving or riding in a car can help release energy. This clearly applied to one man with whom I worked. Whenever he and his partner were trying to work out an issue in their relationship, they would get in the car and take a trip. Within the first hour, all the distracted and built up energy seemed to dissipate and they could get to the core of the issue and find resolution. Also, with an A.D.D. impact, know that your sleep rhythms and needs can be very different and you want to honor them whenever possible.

For you, the support system, do not try to keep up. Let the A.D.D. person go and do what they need in order to stay in balance. If they need to go talk and drive, get in the car. You will get a great deal farther. If they need to sit and play those computer or action games sometimes instead of quietly sitting and talking with you, do not harp. Be glad you have that computer or video game, or they would be driving you crazy. If they come home or return from something on which they had to hyperfocus, especially something that required little or no physical activity, let them unwind first and then talk to them. An hour can make a big difference in their ability to focus on what you need to discuss. Try to remember how tiring hyperfocusing can be.

If you are sharing the bed with them, let them come to bed when they are tired and get up when they are awake, no matter how strange the sleep schedule seems to be. They have their own energy pulses and sleep rhythms that need to be maintained.

Career

Since at least one of the issues that exists in most careers is that of having relationships, much of what I have said in the relationship area can be equally applied to work relationships. As far as careers go, I have a few points to share and/or reiterate, but I am not going to repeat what I just finished saying.

Within the workplace, the A.D.D. individual should utilize all the organizational tools that they are already applying on the home front. Create master checklists and daily checklists, keep a notebook handy at all times, review it daily and give yourself just enough structure to function but not to create boredom.

As far as careers go, either working for yourself or in a position that is very project-orientated are the best options. It will work best if you can work in bursts. To figure out and work within your own rhythms, break when you need to and can work uninterrupted when you are in flow. If you are thinking that I am setting up some tough criteria for your employer, try a smaller company or even a partnership. If you do not want to work for yourself, work in a situation where your gifts, talents and abilities buy you a great deal of leeway. Try to create situations where your brilliance can shine and you can be in joy!

So a job or career where you can jump up and be restless when you need to. As well as you can work at it for twelve hours straight, if that where you are with it. You want structure as what needs to be accomplished, not rigid micro-management.

My message to the adults is be honest, with yourself and to those people who are in your life. Be proud that you have this wonderful gift and be able to know how to use it. Know that the people, in your life, who truly care, will work with you. And the work is definitely worth it.

Chapter 9
Depression

One day, I began to notice a pattern of depression among the people I was working with. At first, I felt that it was probably just related to the isolation, fear, anxiety and shame factors that I addressed in Chapter 6. But then I noticed that the adults who had created techniques to deal with the impacts of the A.D.D. or those who were on medication still tended to lean towards pessimism and could easily fall into obvious depression. The more I looked, the more I saw thought processes and actions that could create or draw depression to them.

I began to look at the love affair with depression. How did it serve them? What made it useful? In the empowerment work I do as a spiritual coach and counselor, I often ask these questions. What I realized was that depression can be a form of self-medicating.

Depression literally depresses or shuts the person down, affecting energy level and motivation. Someone, who is overactive, thinks too much and stands out because of it could easily look *normal* if all those symptoms were *depressed*. I am not saying that the A.D.D. impacted person makes a conscious decision to become and stay depressed; however, because of many of the things that are occurring in their life they are very susceptible to getting depressed. The cycle can begin from there.

The pattern could easily look like the following example. For this example, let us call the individual Katie. Katie, after struggling with feeling outside, different, broken, disabled and in general a problem to the people in her life, finally succumbs to depression. She becomes more subdued. She talks less and is less hyperactive. She may even seem less distracted. She may not be great deal more attentive, but she is less obviously distracted and she is certainly less disruptive. Now, someone with keen insight may approach Katie and ask her if she is OK because she is not acting like herself. On the other hand, she may also be rewarded for what appears as better behavior. Katie may have had a hard time falling asleep or had an irregular sleeping pattern and because of this, getting up in the morning was a real chore. Now she is sleeping more than she ever did and, though she is not thrilled with mornings, she seems to put up fewer struggles about getting up. She appears to have resigned to getting up. In reality, Katie is just feeling too defeated to fight about it.

So, Katie is perceived as doing better and is praised. She starts to feel better and the depression lightens up. Guess what happens? Katie starts perking up. She starts acting more like old Katie. Someone who is really tuned in is likely to welcome back the old, true Katie. However, an equally, if not more likely scenario is one where Katie hears that it was 'too good to last.' She may be asked, "What happened? You were doing so well." Katie prefers the way she was being treated when she was depressed and she may even try to recreate the behavior. Without something suppressing the extra energy, without something suppressing the wonderfully curious and constantly going mind, she is unable to achieve that behavior. She starts feeling hopeless and negative, the depression returns and the cycle has started. After a few times through the cycle, the balance created is that of someone who tends towards pessimism and is mildly depressed or, at the very least, given to depression. That depression then becomes a nice safe, cozy place to hang out. Depending on how big the swings are, this person could easily look manic-depressive. I am not going to say that this happens to every A.D.D. impacted person.

However, it is a scenario that can happen and may happen more than anyone realizes.

One young man with whom I was working often talked about his lifetime struggle with pessimism and depression. He would talk about how he could sleep eighteen hours a day. He wanted a cat's life. Until he would get involved with certain creative projects, those that would require many of his A.D.D. gifts. Then he would become brilliant, outgoing and friendly, functioning on very little sleep for the weeks of the project. His pessimism would disappear and there were no signs of depression. He was allowed to have (and even embraced for) his *artistic temperament*.

When I began working with him, he was in between projects, dealing the best he could in a world that did not allow for the highly energized, artistic temperament. I shared with him my discoveries around the A.D.D., especially the one about depression. I told him that, as we worked with some of the protocols and gave him some new perspectives, he might find that his pessimism and depressive nature would shift. He might even need lees sleep. The thought of sleeping less did not really appeal to him, but the rest of it did, so we gave it a shot. Within six months, he was sleeping less, was more optimistic and was not feeling depressed. He also had not worked on any of the artistic projects that had been a haven for him in the past. He discovered that he could function in both worlds and could allow himself to be artistic everywhere. He could even be a little temperamental—but not detrimentally so.

Oftentimes A.D.D. and depression are linked together, but just as often they are not. The A.D.D. person who is mildly depressed ends up hearing the great pronouncement that they are outgrowing their A.D.D. That could be because the mild depression acts like medication, or perhaps because the person has developed ways to not stand out negatively. The person may have also developed tools to make things work. Inside, they know they have not changed. Maybe they have tried to convince themselves that they have outgrown it, but they know they have not. Whatever the case, look carefully when you examine your life and you are most likely to find depression a companion of your journey. It does not have to be a companion, but it sure has helped—up to this point.

When you cannot determine why you would be depressed, at least not in a way you can express, it is far too easy to decide that it must be chemical or that it must be hereditary and would be best dealt with through medication. Having parts of yourself that you cannot seem to get your hands around makes all kinds of addictions easy—depression being one of those addictions. So if you or a loved one suffers with depression and has A.D.D., think carefully about applying the techniques and perspectives in this book. When you find you have nothing to hide and nothing to be ashamed of you may find depression a less attractive companion.

Chapter 10
Alternatives

Some would say that all the work I do falls into the category of alternative. If one were to define alternative as alternative to drug-based therapy, then I would agree. In this chapter, however, I will be sharing some of the things that I have had personal experience with as well as things that I have come across. Before I go any further, this will be the only chapter that I feel I need to dedicate to someone. This chapter is dedicated to Suzanne Koenig, my research assistant, whose passion for alternatives and thirst for knowledge brought ten times more things to my attention than I would have been sharing with you in this chapter. So thank you, Suzanne, for your passion and commitment to this issue as well as your belief in the 'rightness' of alternatives.

So what I will be presenting to you here are the things that I would recommend checking out. This does not mean that I recommend doing them, but you may want to check them out for yourself. One of my problems with alternatives is that I use them on a case by case basis depending on the information I pick up from the individual I am working with, and they can vary greatly from individual to individual.

Now, as I said earlier, Suzanne brought many alternative techniques for dealing with A.D.D. to my attention. Techniques other than what I was already doing. Some were immediately eliminated because of one of two reasons. Either they claimed to 'cure' a list of things as long as my arm or they approached A.D.D. as something undesirable that it would help eliminate. Therefore, I have chosen to eliminate miracle cures from this section.

The other thing which I feel must be taken into consideration in this section is that sometimes recommendations that I may make or that may work well actually have nothing to do with the A.D.D. impact itself. I address related issues like diet sensitivity and environmental factors—things that may exacerbate the A.D.D., but in most cases are not healthy for anyone in general.

*****

Homeopathy

Homeopathy is a holistic approach to healing which considers the physical, emotional and mental symptoms or patterns of the individual. The body can be brought back into balance and health by stimulating its natural defense mechanisms using 'remedies.' Remedies are mostly derived from animal, plant or mineral sources. They are ingested in pellet, tablet or liquid form and come in various potencies or strengths. Remedies can be used as a preventive measure to strengthen the immune system or when acute or chronic symptoms are manifesting themselves. Homeopathic remedies are nontoxic and do not cause side effects because they are much diluted. They work on a vibrational level. The Food and Drug Administration have accepted homeopathic remedies.

When considering how to manage the 'symptoms' of A.D.D. homeopathically, a consultation with a homeopathic practitioner is recommended. This consultation is much more in depth than those of allopathic practitioners and can take between one and two hours to complete. The homeopath will 'take the case' or gather information about the emotional, mental and physical symptoms by asking questions and observing the client. This information is compared to the symptoms associated with various remedies. Each remedy has a 'picture' of symptoms that it has been known to cure or positively effect. When a match is made between a remedy's picture of symptoms and those symptoms manifesting in the client, this single remedy is given to the client. This is known as 'the law of similars' or like cures like. The client is then monitored for his/her response to the remedy.

RESOURCES:

1. National Center for Homeopathy
   801 North Fairfax Street
   Suite 306
   Alexandria, Virginia 22314
   http://www.homeopathic.org/ Phone: (703) 548-7790
   There is a listing of practitioners that can be searched by name, city, state and country. This website contains a great deal of information.

2. Homeopathic Educational Services
   2124 Kittredge Street
   Berkeley, CA 94704
    Phone: 800-359-9051 (for orders only)
             510-649-0294 (for inquires/catalogs)
   http://www.homeopathic.com
   They sell many, many books, remedy kits and other products. The website has great information and interesting links.

3. Homeopathy: Natural Health Care
   http://homeopathy-cures.com/
   This site is written by Steve and Aviva Waldstein both NDs and classical Homeopaths in Denver Colorado. They have a listing of practitioners by state, something which, is not seen on other lists.

4. Also, do not forget your local bookstore. There are many books available.

*****

Flower Essences

A flower essence is the vibrational (energy) pattern of a flower that brings balance to a person on all levels: physical, emotional, mental and spiritual. Placing the flower's petals in a bowl of clean water and setting them in the sun for about three hours makes a flower essence. This releases the specific healing and balancing pattern of the flower into the water in a very condensed form. The petals are removed, and this tincture is diluted and preserved with brandy. The essence is taken orally a few drops at a time.

Flower essences help to heal, balance and strengthen our electrical energy system. Our electrical system can become short-circuited or shut down as we go through life. Unless this is corrected, our bodies can be cut off from the electrical life force energy they need to be healthy and may experience pain, illness or disease. The electrical system can also overload, which may cause hyperactivity and twitching. Essences are able to reconnect and rebalance the circuitry in the body. Since people with A.D.D. seem to have very well developed nervous systems, are very sensitive to energy and tend to overload energetically, they can greatly benefit from using flower essences. Flower essences also address the mental and emotional patterns in our etheric bodies, which contain our destructive mental, spiritual and emotional illusions or blocks. These blocks vibrate at a slow rate. Because the essences vibrate at a higher rate, they help to facilitate the release of these blocks. When our blocks are released, we can open ourselves more to receive the healing energies of Spirit.

Flower essences are extremely safe. If a person does ingest an essence his/her body does not need, the pattern is released. There are no known side effects at all. They are extremely powerful, yet extremely gentle.

RESOURCES:
1. Bach Flower Remedies, Ltd
    Website: http://www.bachflower.com
    Bach flower remedies can usually be purchased at
    most health food stores.

2. Bach Center
    Website: http://www.bachcenter.com
    Here you will find information on the Bach flower
    remedies and can purchase them.

3. Green Hope Farm, Molly Sheehan
    POB 125
    True Road
    Meriden, NH 03770
    Phone: 603-469-3662
    They produce and sell many, many flower essences.

4. Perelandra, LTD: co-founder, Machaelle Wright
    P.O. Box 3603
    Warrenton, VA 20188
    Phone: 1-800-960-8806
    Website: www.perelandra-ltd.com/index.htm
    They produce and sell flower essences. They also have
    various publications concerning their use.

*****

Biofeedback / Neurofeedback

Biofeedback is a process in which information on how a
person's body and brain are working is amplified and shown to
that person. For example, various devices are used to measure
muscle tension and body temperature which help people learn to
regulate their blood pressure, temperature and other physical and
mental functions that are not usually consciously controlled.
Biofeedback is used to treat stress-related conditions like migraine

headaches and chronic pain.

Neurofeedback is a form of biofeedback also referred to as an EEG biofeedback. It uses an electroencephalograph to train a person to alter his/her brain wave patterns. Electrodes are placed on the scalp which sense brain wave activity. There is no pain associated with this and no electricity goes into the brain. The brain wave information is sent into a computer, which translates them into pictures. The person is able to change his/her brain waves by watching how these brain waves effect the pictures on the computer. Computer games for children are now available which require the use of mind power alone to play. The child learns to affect the game by increasing or decreasing certain brain waves. In effect, Neurofeedback retrains the brain to produce the desired brain waves. There are four different kinds of brain waves:

Delta: .5-4cycles/second or .5-4hertz(HZ): Deep sleep
Theta: 4-8HZ: Dreamy, deep meditation
Alpha: 8-12HZ: Calm, mentally unfocused, relaxed wakefulness
Beta: 12-15HZ: Alert concentration, normal waking state up to 35HZ. High beta, excited, anxious

Studies have shown that boys and girls with A.D.H.D. produce more theta brain waves and less beta waves than children without A.D.H.D.[1] do. Neurofeedback teaches children and adults to control their minds so that they can increase the amount of beta waves they produce while decreasing the theta waves. Therefore, they are more able to focus their attention and concentration.

It takes about 40-80 sessions (40-60minutes per session) or as some sources {eegspectrum.com} say 20-40 sessions, to produce lasting EEG and clinical changes. Follow-up assessments should be done at about 1 month, 6 months and 1 year after the treatment is complete. [2]

---

[1] "Attention Deficit Hyperactivity, Disorder: Neurological Basis and Treatment Alternatives". (www.snrjnt.org)

[2] "ADHD: Neurological Basis and Treatment Alternatives". www.snr-jnt.org

Follow-up studies on children who have received Neurofeedback training have shown significant increases in academic and behavior scores. Some children have advanced up to 2 ½ years in grade level achievement and have increased IQ scores by as much as 15points[3].

RESOURCES:
1. *Journal of Neurotherapy*
   Website: www.snr-jnt.org/
   This site has reprints of all major articles and a list of Neurotherapy providers in the U.S. and the world.

2. *Neurofeedback Research and Clinical Services*
   Website: www.eegspectrum.com/
   There is a lot of information on this site. It includes a list of recommended books, articles, providers, etc.

3. *Sterman-Kaiser Imaging Laboratory*
   Website: www.skiltopo.com/
   This site had interesting articles and recommended books.

4. *EEG Biofeedback/Neurofeedback Central*
   Website: www.futurehealth.org/nfcntral.htm.
   This site has some interesting links.

*****

Nutritional Approaches for A.D.D.

Blue-green algae and essential fatty acids are two nutritional supplements that I recommend to my clients. Blue-green algae is a super food rich in vitamins, chelated minerals and trace minerals. It is a concentrated source of beta-carotene and is one

---

[3] "Wired for Miracles" by John Robbins March/April, 1996 on www.eggspectrum.com

of the highest sources of chlorophyll. It consists of up to 69% of balanced high quality vegetable protein and it contains all eight essential amino acids. The body uses these to create complete proteins. Rare and essential fatty acids, such as Omega 3's, are also contained in blue-green algae. It is a blood purifier and a powerful antiseptic that seeks out and eliminates toxins (free radicals) in the body.

For more information on blue-green algae, see:

1. www.spirulina.com.
2. www.The-peoples.net/celltech

Essential fatty acids (EFA'S) are necessary for health. Except for Omega-3 and Omega 6, the body makes all of them. These fats are especially needed for the healthy functioning of the heart, brain and cell membranes.[4] A deficiency of EFAs can result in numerous physical problems as well as the 'symptoms' of A.D.D. Good sources of EFAs are cold water fish and flaxseed oil for Omega-3's and leafy green vegetables, borage oil, evening primrose oil, black current oil, and flaxseed oil for Omega-6's. Also, do not forget the blue green algae. Which may end up being the best source as Omega 3 oils need proteins, vitamins and minerals in adequate amounts of zinc, vitamins E, C, and B-6 (all of which are in blue-green algae) to convert Omega 6 acids to Omega 3's.

According to several sources, most of us are not getting the required amounts of essential fatty acids our bodies need. One reason is the trans-fatty acids we consume. Trans-fatty acids are formed when polyunsaturated oils are hydrogenated and/or heated at high temperature. Trans-fatty acids interfere with the functioning of EFA acids. Mostly, we ingest trans-fatty acids from margarine and shortenings made from partially hydrogenated vegetable oils. These margarine and shortenings are found in most processed foods as, breads, crackers, cookies, potato chips,

---

[4] Natural *Treatments for ADD and Hyperactivity* by Skye Weintraub, N.D., p.110

peanut butter and fried foods. Read the labels on foods and notice whether they contain hydrogenated or partially hydrogenated oils. Also, note that Holland has banned the sale of margarine containing trans-fatty acids. For more detailed information on EFAs and trans-fatty acids see:

1.   *Natural Treatments for ADD and Hyperactivity* by Skye Weintraub, N.D.

2.   *Born to Explore* at www.borntoexplore.org/omega.htm. Here you will find an article "ADDers Are More Likely to Have Fatty Acids Deficiencies" The author sites other resources, two of which are:

    a)   *Smart Fats: How Dietary Fats and Oils Affect Mental, Physical and Emotional Intelligence* by Michael A. Schmidt.
    b)   *The Omega Plan* by Artemis P. Simopoulos, M.D. and Jo Robinson, 1998.

*****

Herbal Approaches To A.D.D.

Herbalists were the original health care practitioners. They became our original doctors and they have been the keepers of much wisdom when it comes to the harmonious running of all four of our bodies. If I can find something that will alleviate, promote, or remedy that which nature itself took the time, energy and love to create, herbalism will always be my first choice. One of the best all around sources for information is the *Prescription for Nutritional Healing* by James F. Balch, N.D. and Phyllis A. Balch, C.N.C. If there are out of balances occurring, check there first and seek out the natural ways to achieve balance. In addition, meeting with a good herbalist can be a very positive life changing experience, provided you follow through with the recommendations! One herbal combination that I found which has worked quite powerfully is an herbal combination of L-Tyrosine, B Complex and Spirulina. Before you go running out and by bottles of each do the research for yourself and see if it feels correct for you.

Again, I am not telling any of you to just begin doing this. See a qualified herbal health practitioner or do the research, then decide if you would like to try it.

*****

Diet

There are whole books written on diet that touch upon, if not focus on, the A.D.D. In doing the scans, I often times will find sensitivities to drugs, alcohol, caffeine, dairy, and sometimes even wheat. This is not to say that everyone who is impacted with the A.D.D. will have any or all these sensitivities, but they are things to watch out for. A diet rich in whole foods, organic, lightly cooked or raw foods is always a good bet. Eliminating things with food coloring and dyes is highly suggested. Eliminating foods heavily processed with lots of chemicals also tends to make a big difference.

Now here is a little secret I would like to share. Do not try to make many big diet changes all at once. Especially if you, or your child, who is use to a diet that is not good for them. As things start coming out of the diet, find good tasting alternatives to work into the diet. The change is much less likely to become sabotaged. Sometimes you need to keep clear in your mind what you are doing for yourself or for your child. If someone handed you or your child a really great tasting berry, and as you started eating it, told you that in certain quantities that it was poisonous, would you keep eating it, just because it tasted good? Would you keep feeding it to your child? Would you do it because it was easy? Or because they were going to complain if they did not get anymore? If you or your child is eating something which you are having an allergic reaction to, which is toxic to your body why would you keep eating it?

Remember, if you are having negative side effects that are increasing what would be normal aspects of your A.D.D. to unmanageable proportions, then you are having an allergic reaction to that kind of food. Understand that. Also make sure your child and anybody feeding your child understands that, including family, school and anyone who maybe feeding your child. Do not let it become dismissed as 'another wacky thing you're doing' or they are just a child a little of this or that will not hurt them. Think of that poison berry every time you want to give in.

I recommend cleaning up diet by eliminating, or at the very least reducing refined white sugar, artificial colors, artificial flavors, artificial sweeteners, preservatives, phosphates and of course hydrogenated oils. The *Feingold Diet* recommends, in addition to everything listed above, the elimination of food additives and caffeine. In *Helping Your Hyperactive/ADD Child,* John Taylor discusses his experiences using the *Feingold Diet* with his clients.

Information on Feingold diet, as well as other diet suggestions can be found at:

1. For the *Feingold Diet* www.feingold.org/index.html
2. *The ADD/ADHD Online Newsletter* at www.nlci.com/nutrition/newsuse.htm
3. And on www.csprint.org you will find a *Parent's Guide to Diet, ADHD and Behavior,* as well as other reports that may be of interest in this area.

*****

Energy Work and A.D.D.

I have given both my children and my adults energy work in the form of Wei Chi Tibetan Reiki™, with positive results. I also create meditation and shielding tapes, which have helped. I also teach my clients breathing and centering exercises. These are all tools I can teach my clients to do on their own and they help manage the times of excess energy or mental over load. Some of my clients have benefited by taking a martial art, Tai Chi or yoga class. If you are looking for shielding mediations, I recommend the book *Invisible Armor: Protecting Your Personal Energy* or get the CD *Creating Your Invisible Armor*. Both are by Thomas Hensel.

*****

A.D.D. and Indigo

Since beginning this work, I am often asked about the term 'indigo child' and whether I have read the book *The Indigo Children* by Lee Carroll and Jan Tober. My response was always the same: "No." I stayed away from reading other people's works as much as possible while I was still in the creation stage of this book. I left it up to my research assistant, Suzanne, to weed out and highlight anything I really needed to see that would help my work. She repeatedly told me that I needed to read the book. Finally, when I was on the last legs of writing this book, I was drawn to read *The Indigo Children*. The premise of the book is about a new kind of children who are being born, children who appear to the author as indigo in color and who are here to bring us into a new reality. It is an interesting book and I like some of what it says, but parts of it cause me concern. I do feel, however, that the authors' intentions were not all that far away from my own: recognizing an evolutionary change in our species, which is showing up more and more in the form of our children.

Comparing the messages and approaches by which they classify indigo children with my own approaches leads me to see that we are, in many ways, talking about the same group. The indigo child, as I understand their description, is a subgroup of what I am seeing as the A.D.D. impacted child. The major differences lie in the levels that are most impacted.

The indigo children are clearly more obviously impacted on the spiritual and intellectual levels. They appear to be only mildly impacted on the emotional and physical levels. In addition, some of the children who were highlighted within that group had the more obvious qualities because of the environment in which they were being raised. They were being **allowed** to be more spiritually aware and in touch. I also suspect that the support systems around them were more aware of diet, environment and how the children were approached and treated. Therefore, some of the factors that may exacerbate qualities that we classify as A.D.D. were minimized.

Would I recommend reading *The Indigo Chil*dren? Yes. It definitely shares some interesting insights and helps bring many of our children who are different into a better, more positive light. Would I separate A.D.D. impacted children from indigo children? No. I really do feel that the indigo child I read about is simply someone who displays a few of the many ways that the gift of A.D.D. manifests itself.

What are my concerns? Taking those children who are less impacted in social, educationally-acceptable ways and making them different and better than the rest leaves the children who are impacted in the more obvious ways still waiting for the Ritalin (drug) noose to tighten. The bottom line is this: all children are special and no child should have their personality and their uniqueness lost in a drug haze.

Chapter 11
Hopes, Fears and Final Words

Hopes, fears and final words. At least these will be the final words for this book. Just for the sake of confusion, I have decided that I want to talk about fears first, then hopes and then add my closing thoughts. I knew this when I titled this chapter, but I did not like the energy of a chapter named 'Fears, Hopes and Final Words.' It seemed to put the emphasis on the wrong places since I really see this book as more about hope than fear. There is enough fear and ignorance around the A.D.D. impacted person as it is. But I do have a few fears of what has occurred or what could transpire with mishandling.

Fears

The concept of brilliant, angry, isolated people who can be emotionally detached scares me. Every time I hear about some atrocity coming from our children, I wonder—especially about the ones who showed brilliant insight and planning in their acts of violence. While the world wonders what could provoke such an almost compassionless act, I wonder about the pressure cooker we have created for these children who are different; the children we label, ostracize, isolate, medicate and force into situations where they just do not fit. What happens to their hate? Their anger? How do they strike back? What happens if they decide to stop taking the zombifying medication and become more of who they are? Do they come back with pieces missing?

When people talk of monsters, I ask who or what was the Dr. Frankenstein that created them? Are we, the people who chose to deny their right to be unique special beings, the creators? Are we, the pill pushers, the creators? Are we, the axes who try to cut them into the size pieces that are easiest to fit in the box and are easiest for us, the Dr. Frankenstein? I wonder. This is not to say that every person/child who commits a crime is A.D.D., nor is this the way that every person with A.D.D. will act. But even if a few do, have we still not been their creators?

It scares me to breed generations of children who think that pills are the answer, that uniqueness is a bad thing and that life is all about fitting in, not being who you are. I cannot believe it sends a positive message to our children to say that a pill is acceptable as long as it eliminates what is not popular or desirable. Is this a different variation of the kind of messages we sent which led to hundreds of thousands of girls to develop eating disorders, or young men to take steroids? It scares me to create the idea that what is easiest for everyone else is what is best for the individual.

Another of my concerns is the potential loss we face through the limiting of these brilliant, gifted and talented individuals. What kind of price will our future and our future generations pay for our taking the easy way out? Have we not already put enough burdens upon our future generations? They are inheriting a polluted, over-populated, over-harvested planet loaded with toxic waste and a disappearing ozone layer. Is that not bad enough without slowing their ability to recover from our follies and our sins by medicating away their brilliant minds so that we can shove a few more kids in a classroom or make a little more wealth in our lifetime? Will they thank us for the extra wealth when they are stuck with a planet that is beyond repair? I have always liked that bumper sticker that says some variation of 'I cannot wait for the day when the schools do not have to beg for money and the military needs to have bake sales to build bombs.'

Finally, there is an organization called C.H.A.D.D. (Children & Adults with Attention Deficit Disorders) that scares me. It scares me because the majority of its early funding came from the drug company that produces Ritalin, the number one drug of choice for A.D.D. This fact does not appear in its literature. From all the evidence I can find, C.H.A.D.D. supports only treatment plans or ideologies that include the use of drugs and has been dismissive of other approaches. It scares me because C.H.A.D.D. puts itself out as the best and largest resource for information and guidance for families who have children with A.D.D., yet I have seen no evidence of different points of view that allow the parents to choose. In fact, C.H.A.D.D. guides parents into programs and ways of thinking which are clearly most beneficial for the drug company that financially supports them. Have they done anything legally wrong? No. Morals and ethics are other matters, but no one ever said these were the same things. If they clearly let everyone know about or were more receptive to treatment styles that were not medicine-based, I would be more forgiving. But, as they stand now, they scare me.

I have heard that they do provide some good services and definitely have brought some goods things to the A.D.D. community, but their omissions, questionable loyalties, and narrowness make me and keep me suspicious of the purity of their motives. The fact that they are allowed to put things up in the schools scares me, but perhaps the schools, the drug company and C.H.A.D.D. are not strange bedfellows. That scares me the most.

But … I have some hopes, too.

Hopes

I am hopeful when I look into the faces of these children and know that the future can be safe because they can go where we could not. They can see and be their spiritual selves. Intellectually, they can take us where we have never been and if we let them, they will do it with heart and soul, something we often kept at arm's length. Emotionally, they will not be slaves to or make others the victims of their emotions, if we teach them how to manage those emotions. Moreover, they will have the energy to make these things happen.

These things make me hopeful, as do some of the parents who stand up and say, "No." In addition, the visionary teachers and other professionals who are trying to be the conscience to which we often avoid listening give me hope. You will find that my hopes take up much less space than my fears, but this is because the whole book is a book of hope.

Final Words

What more can I say? Plenty. But it is time for this book to end. As I continue my work, I will continue to share what I discover so that all may benefit from it if they choose. That is what it is all about when you hit the bottom line: choice. So, as you move away from this book and these ideas, choose wisely. Never forget what is at stake. Every day we make thousands of choices. What will you choose?

If you are choosing for a child ask yourself, "In twenty years will this child thank me for the choices I made on this issue?" I have often seen comparisons that taking a drug for A.D.D. is like taking a drug for diabetes or for epilepsy. It is not the same and never let anyone tell you it is. Your child's life is not at stake because of A.D.D. In fact, many people still argue that A.D.D. is a fictional, created condition. Your child takes medications for A.D.D. not because it helps him or her to live, but because it makes them easier to manage. Never underestimate the price they pay for it.

Be well, choose wisely and plan for a future that looks better than the one we have received.

Additional Bibliography

Carroll, Lee & Jan Tober, *The Indigo Children*, Hay House, 1999.

"Frequently Asked Questions," Neurofeedback Research and Clinical Services, at: www.eegspectrum.com.

Lubar, Joel F., Ph.D. and Judith O. Lubar, LCSW, BCD, "Attention Deficit Hyperactivity Disorder: Neurological Basis and Treatment Alternatives*", Journal of Neurotherapy* at www.snr-jnt.org.

Robbins, John, "Wired for Miracles," March/April, 1996. (See: *Neurofeedback Research and Clinical Services* at ww.eegspectrum.com.

Sheehan, Molly. *Flower Essences: A Guide to Green Hope Farm.* Green Hope Farm, 1999.

The Merrow Report, *Attention Deficit Disorder: A Dubious Diagnosis?*, Learning Inc., 1995. (See: www.pbs.org/merrow/repository/ Television/Past/~attn/guide.html)

Walker, Sydney, MD. *The Hyperactivity Hoax.* St. Martin's Press, 1998.

Weintraub, Skye, N.D. *Natural Treatments For ADD and Hyperactivity.* Woodland Publishing, 1997.

Wright, Machaelle, *Flower Essences: Reordering Our Understanding and Approach to Illness and Health*, Perelandra, LTD, 1988.

Recommended Websites

About Attention Deficit Disorder: www.add.miningco.com/health/add
   Many, many, many subjects to click on relating to ADD/ ADHD, including   information concerning children, teens, and adults. Much information on   alternative treatments.

ADD Action Group: http://www.addgroup.org
   A non-profit organization helping people find alternatives for ADD as well as other disabilities. They have articles on various alternative approaches to ADD, recommended book list, Round Table television show, and news articles.

The ADD/ADHD Online Newsletter: www.nlci.com/nutrition
   Information on nutrition, including recommended books and web links.

ADHD News.com: www.adhdnews.com/
   This site includes: "Advocating for Your Child ": links and information, "ADDed Attractions": a free monthly e-mail mailing, recommended books, many links, "Special Ed. Rights and Responsibilities," and great articles.

Ask About ADD: www.azstarnet.com/~ask/
   This site has too many interest subjects with an extremely large amount of information to list. See for yourself. Extensive site index.

Born to Explore: www.borntoexplore.org
   Great information on essential fatty acids, diet and food additives, many books listed with many descriptions, and many interesting links.

Center for Science in the Public Interest: www.cspinet.org
   Information on nutrition, food safety, and food additives. Scroll down to "ADHD Report and Parent's Guide": includes

scientist's letters to the department of Health and Human Services, and diet.

Center for the Study of Psychiatry and Psychology: www.breggin.com
    Information on Dr. Breggin's books, articles on drugs, and on legal cases.

Child Development Institute: www.cdipage.com/adhd.htm
    This site has much information on drugs, current research on ADD, diet and nutrition.

Doctor's Guide: www.docguide.com
    Click on "Select a Channel" and choose "psychiatry other" for information related to ADD, or research a specific drug. Many articles on drugs, as well as up to date articles on all health topics.

Holistic Resource Center: www.holisticmed.com/
    Click on "Disease and Disabilities Resources" for information on ADD. Other sections include: books, articles: visiting experts presentations, current news on various health issues, and case histories for various health issues.

IDEA (Individuals with Disabilities Education Act):
    www.ed.gov/offices/OSERS/IDEA/
    Information on the law itself can be downloaded. There is general information, an overview, summary, and questions & answers. Also available is the IDEA 97 Training Package which has information on some of the legal requirements and provisions.

Journal of Neurotherapy: www.snr-jnt.org/index.htm
    You will find a list of SNR members who are neurofeedback providers listed by country and state in alphabetical order, "Neurofeedback Archive: articles, and links, as well as other information.

Mental Health Net: mentalhelp.net/
    Included here are a listing of ADHD/ADD support organizations, listing of providers, and many links.

Natural Health and Longevity Resource Center: www.all-natural.com
    There are articles, health and nutrition products, health news: links to various publications and their health sections, and "Leading Edge Research and Technical Subject Index: a way to research information on a specific subject.

Neurofeedback Research and Clinical Services: www.eegspectrum.com
    Explains what neurofeedback is, has a list of providers worldwide, specific information on ADHD/ADD plus many other "disorders," FAQ about neurofeedback, scientific articles, research programs, research news: announcements, media discussion, recommended books, mental news, and many articles.

Office of Civil Rights: www.ed.gov/offices/OCR
    Information on how to file a discrimination complaint. Including a listing by state of their enforcement offices, what their procedures are, how complaints are evaluated, resolves, etc. They also have many links.

Outside the Box: home.att.net/~adhd.kids/
    New articles and links (information for college bound students), announcements, information specifically for teachers and for parents, links, and much more.

Parent Training and Information Centers: www.taalliance.org
    These centers provide training and information to parents and professionals who work with children and youth with disabilities. You will find web links and resources, updates on legislative issues regarding special education, urgent "What's New" section, and a listing by state of Parent Centers by state.

RX Med: www.rxmed.com

Click on "drug monographs for all medications"- very extensive listing. The monographs give much information.

Taming the Triad: www.tamingthetriad.com

The "In the News" is current. The Q & A section is organized according to subject, and there are many great links.

Thom Hartman: www.thomhartman.com

You will find information on his books, a free e-mail newsletter, and many links: including the Hunters School for children with ADD.

About The Author

Dr. Kevin Ross Emery, a resident of New Hampshire, maintains a full-time coaching and counseling practice, focussing on alternative approaches for dealing with Attention Deficit Disorder. He is a cutting-edge practitioner whose career has spanned several different worlds. He began his career in the corporate world as trainer, trouble-shooter and manager. Dr. Emery has worked for such organizations as Dartmouth College, Hilton, Sheraton and American Express. He also spent time in the community service field working to create a program to help people with disabilities mainstream into the community at-large.

Dr. Emery started his own business in the early nineties, working as a spiritual coach and counselor, teacher, business consultant and hands-on healer. He is the founder of Synergy Business Consulting™. Among their many offerings, Dr. Emery and his partner Dr. Thomas A. Hensel are also the creators and teachers of the *Wei Chi Tibetan Reiki*™ system of natural healing. Dr. Emery holds a B.A. in Business & Psychology from the University of New Hampshire and both a Masters and Doctorate in Divinity from the Universal Brotherhood University.

Dr. Emery is the author of the *LightLines* titles *Managing The Gift: Alternative Approaches For Attention Deficit Disorder* and *Combing The Mirror (and other steps in your spiritual path)*. He is the co-author of the three audio tapes *Prosperity & Manifestation*, *The Lost Steps of Reiki* and *The Channeled Teachings of Simon Peter*, as well as the two books *The Lost Steps of Reiki: The Channeled Teachings of Wei Chi* and *Experiment Earth: Journey Back To The Beginning*.

To contact Dr. Kevin Ross Emery . . .

Dr. Kevin Ross Emery
c/o LightLines Publishing
PO Box 5067
Portsmouth, NH 03802-5067

(603) 433-5784
FAX (603) 766-5786
E-mail: *The Add Gift@aol.com*

And visit his website:
www.weboflight.com/ADD.htm